For my Father, **Murison Robertson**, with all my love

THIS IS A CARLTON BOOK

Design and special photography
copyright © 2000 Carlton Books Limited
Text copyright © 2000 Hilary Robertson
This edition was published by Carlton Books Limited in 2000
20 Mortimer Street, London W1T 3JW

A CIP catalogue record for this book is available from the
British Library
ISBN 1 84222 067 5

Printed and bound in Dubai

Editorial Manager: **Venetia Penfold**

Art Director: **Penny Stock**

Senior Art Editor: **Barbara Zuñiga**

Project Editor: **Zia Mattocks**

Designer: **Liz Lewis at LewisHallam**

Copy Editors: **Lisa Dyer and Jane Donovan**

Picture Researcher: **Abi Dillon**

Special Photography: **Mel Yates and Tom Leighton**

Production Manager: **Garry Lewis**

Boudoir

CREATING THE BEDROOM OF YOUR DREAMS

Hilary Robertson

CARLTON
BOOKS

contents

Romantic

Sexy

Exotic

*A*s a child I was obsessed by two things: my dolls and my mother's magazines. I couldn't really see the point of being a child at all, disinterested as I was in playing games with balls and mud and tearing about on bicycles. My interests were more precocious, to say the least, and therefore my dolls led the most sophisticated lives I could invent for them. They were Supermodels before Supermodels even existed, flitting between London, New York and Paris on 'assignments', courted by square-jawed 'Ken' dolls with Aston Martins and St Tropez tans. Of course, I didn't actually know anyone remotely like this in leafy suburbia, but I gleaned all the information I needed to know from the magazines I read.

The nerve centre of my finishing school for dolls was my bedroom and my friends' bedrooms. In the pink candlewick intimacy of these dens, my stable of 'lovelies' was cosseted and preened to prepare them for forays into the world of international glamour. Tucked away in our little girls' boudoirs, we could indulge our secret fantasies and escape from eavesdropping grown-ups. By extension, the place where I now sleep, dream and dress is a retreat from the demands of the 'real world', away from work and logic-driven design concepts – no monastic minimalism for me!

Boudoir-style, a look that recently emerged from the fashion catwalks, is an explosion of ultra-romantic floral, embroidered, be-ribboned, laced and frilled costumes. Dressing-up box clothes became a hit with women who were tired of sportswear and slick, understated uniforms, and bored by the no-frills grip of minimalism. Suddenly, they can't get enough of sequinned Fendi baguette bags, flimsy satin mules and tiny, jewel-like evening purses. Frivolity is back!

In the 1990s, encouraged by Ikea and the Scandinavian blond-wood posse, you may have 'chucked out your chintz', but you may be prepared to take a fresh look at it now. *Boudoir* is all about realizing your style fantasies, whether they first germinated in your girlish, childhood bedroom or were inspired by exotic travels abroad. You can afford to decorate a private space, seen by few other people, in an expressive, quixotic style. Assemble a few of your favourite things – a painting, a precious stone, a postcard, a pair of shoes – and go from there. Define your decorating persona.

Fortunately, my twin obsessions developed into a career as a stylist and contributor to some of the most beautiful lifestyle publications, but I'm convinced that the concept for this book really began with my dolls and the magazines, and my 10-year-old imagination.

romantic

Material girl

The material girl has never graduated from childhood's dressing-up phase. She keeps hats in hatboxes and delicates in tissue paper, and sleeps with her new shoes on her pillow. She likes nothing better than to scour flea markets and thrift shops for crepe de Chine slips or floral tea dresses. Her magpie instincts draw her towards anything decorative or glittery and she shows her prizes off in her boudoir. Material girl is more likely to hang a particularly delicious frock on the wall than tuck it away in a wardrobe, perhaps taking her lead from fashion designer Betsey Johnson, who hangs her exquisite dresses in a row at her window instead of curtains. She is even prepared to buy clothes that do not fit her and will never actually be worn. A hopelessly impractical but 'sublime' beaded slipper becomes part of a still life on the dressing table; an organza confection strewn with velvet roses looks perfect floating above the bed and was never intended to be worn either.

There is something paradoxically fashionable and timeless about this look, which some people have adopted for ages. The material girl learned to love vintage dressing from her mother and grandmother, who imbued her with a healthy respect for design classics; an impeccable pigskin Hermès Kelly bag has been passed down through the female line. She started planning her boudoir on a shopping trip to one of those romantic little fashion boutiques. The room she imagined was to be a mini version of the boutique – sensually dark, dressed in cobweb laces and devoré velvets and drowning in ostrich-feather fans and costume jewellery.

Magnetically drawn to any emporium that thoroughly celebrates the feminine, she has made Tocca her new shrine. Her lust for sugared-almond hued broderie anglaise bed linen knows no bounds, and she is more than happy to dry-clean her pillow cases.

'customize
and embellish'

the material girl's mantra

style signature

Material girl delights in detail; no heel is too kittenish, no slip too diaphanous, no rose print too blowsy for her tastes. Fondant shades of pistachio, lilac, duck-egg blue and sugared-almond pink are mixed and matched with abandon.

She dresses her bed with the same attention as she would dress herself. Plain white or matching sets of linen are declared 'too boring'; only an ensemble of deftly coordinated 'separates' will do. An antique-satin, quilted eiderdown with Tocca's delicately embroidered crepe pillow cases and monogrammed linen sheets is just one of endless combinations. Old-fashioned merino-wool blankets with satin edges and brushed-cotton candy-striped sheets make her instantly nostalgic.

Brutal minimalism unnerves her – all empty space, hard edges and 'nothing to look at'. She wants to display her clever finds, not shut them away. Her instinct is always to soften. Technology (ugly, modern and masculine) is hidden away in a French armoire. Chairs, sofas and tables wear their own costumes and are decorated with loose covers, scarves, throws and cushions. Drawers and the insides of cupboards are lined with pretty rosy wallpaper or decoupage from magazines. Her television has been painted lilac. She is meticulous in her sense of detail. No surface escapes her attention.

The look has a guaranteed individualism. Material girl loves to customize, to add touches of her own. An ordinary plain cotton sheet can always be dyed, embroidered, be-ribboned or beaded to give it the maximum decorative appeal. A piece of fabric from a worn-out garment can be added to a cushion or throw as a border or panel.

In summer the material girl extends her boudoir style to the garden. Alfresco entertaining involves bringing her antique French sofa and Aubusson rug into the garden, along with lace, tulle and flower-trimmed lamps. Tables are swathed in tapestries and antique linen tablecloths, and laden with exotic fruits, candles and storm lanterns, as well as her best silver cutlery. Such extravagant picnics would not look out of place in the lushness of a Merchant Ivory film.

get the look

walls

Every scheme starts with one decision which informs every other one along the way. If you choose a patterned wallpaper, all your accessories and fabrics will have to work around it – and this takes confidence. Instead, wallpaper can be used in small quantities on only one wall, inside an armoire or beneath a dado rail, but keep to a limited palette for consistency. The easiest solution is to paint walls off-white or pastel shades and keep the drama for the bed and curtains. If you choose to paper your walls, keep to a muted spot, stripe or trellis design.

furniture

Whether real antiques or lovingly revived junk, furniture must be curvaceous with an air of frivolity. A dressing table is an absolute necessity. Where else is she to assemble her ever-expanding collection of decorative hair clips, exquisitely bottled lotions and potions and a panoply of other fripperies? A dressing table can be effectively contrived from a console-sized table, covered in fabric (no need to sew, just use a staple gun) and topped with glass and a mirror on a stand. Inexpensive kidney-shaped tables made of chipboard should be fitted with a skirt or valance in something fresh and jaunty, like broderie anglaise or gingham. Screens, hatboxes, dressmaker's dummies and milliner's blocks are all useful props for containing or displaying paraphernalia. Find them at flea markets or in shops that specialize in retail display. A gorgeous twirly-girly bed, most probably French and antique, is the most important investment – the curvy shape is key to the look. Freshen up sombre dark wood with a lick of paint or lime wash, or try painting a traditional metal frame an unexpected colour.

soft furnishings

Choose dress materials rather than traditional furnishing fabrics for curtains and bed coverings. Mix East with West, Tocca-style, by combining cherry blossom embroidery with broderie anglaise, a Liberty print or an unglazed chintz.

how to

'Cartonnage' is a way of using humble cardboard to create decorative effects. The elaborate white chair (above and right), a pastiche of the Louis style, started life as plain, brown-stained bentwood. Designer Kerry Skinner completely transformed it with strips of corrugated cardboard fashioned into flourishes and curlicues.

1. Using reference pictures of curved furniture details, sketch out the basic design that you have chosen for your chair.

2. Cut out strips of corrugated cardboard and bend them into shapes, experimenting with their position on the chair. Finally, glue them in place.

3. Make an imitation gesso by mixing ½ litre (1 pint) of white exterior paint with 1 tablespoon of all-purpose filler and 1 tablespoon of fine paper-pulp mix. Paint the chair with two coats.

4. When dry, paint the chair with white water-based paint. Finish with subtle touches of acrylic gold paint, then seal with water-based varnish.

Outfit the bed with luxurious sheets and a duvet or quilt, and accessorize with 'bed scarves' – flimsy pieces of decorative embroidered or beaded silk organza. A plain cotton sheet can be transformed with a deep, decorative border at the top. Double-sided curtains are ideal for fickle material girls. Back plain-coloured lengths with patterns, checks, stripes or florals and turn them when you tire of one side. Hang the curtains from simple poles with large clips.

lights

Chandeliers and wall sconces with crystal drops are the prettiest way to light the boudoir. Clear and coloured glass drops, available from lighting specialists, can be added to a simple frame. Inexpensive Indian beaded shades can be bought, or plain ones decorated with feathers, sequins or ribbons. Candlesticks are an elegant way to create a soft, romantic mood or decorate the bed or mirror with a string of floral electric lights.

'How lovely – green velvet and silver, I call that a dream, so soft and delicious, too.' She rubbed a fold of the skirt against her cheek. 'Mine's a silver lamé, it smells like a birdcage when it gets hot but I do love it. Aren't you thankful evening skirts are long again?'

Nancy Mitford, *Love in a Cold Climate*

Ice queen

The ice queen seeks serenity and light in her private retreat. She is
a dedicated disciple of the one-colour colour scheme – there is no need for dramatic design
statements, the subtlety of the scheme is statement enough. She regards 'whiteness' as a
state of mind and understands why the Eskimos have 500 words for snow; there are just as
many shades of white in her ethereal boudoir. Addicted to purity, tranquillity and spirituality,
she finds that living in a space with gentle, ambient light, where nothing jars or demands too
much attention, frees her mind. Her 'ice palace' is a blissfully forgiving, endless white space,
which has a soothing, transcendental effect on all who enter it.

The ice queen adopts a ritualistic approach to maintaining her environment. She takes
enormous pleasure in filling her linen cupboard with properly ironed and folded antique
monogrammed bed linen, waffle towels, Egyptian-cotton sheets, merino-wool blankets and
polar-fleece throws. Her laundry is scented with French *eau de linge* and displayed with all
the self-consciousness of a contemporary art installation.

Simple things have always given her aesthetic pleasure – a glass of milk, a paper cup,
new plimsolls, a snowdrop. She collects chalky pebbles, feathers, sea shells – objects with soul –
and arranges still lifes on windowsills and side tables. The mistress of restraint, she is liberated
from the confusion that dogs most peoples lives: if it's not white or sheer, it doesn't stay. She
has even been known to re-cover all her books in plain white dust jackets. Fashions may
change, but the ice queen will always be able to update her bedroom by introducing new
accessories – an assortment of white porcelain tea cups, a group of white milk jugs, some
antique lace petticoats or a collection of white shirts.

style signature

White is not as impractical as you might think. The ice queen loves the utilitarian elegance of fashion designer Ann Demeulemeester's long work table, tightly covered in white canvas and secured with upholstery tacks; when it becomes grubby, it can be painted with water-based paint. A one-colour scheme is a forgiving one for 'ordinary' furniture and accessories, as it cannot fail to look sophisticated. The ice queen dresses herself as she does her home, realizing she looks unnervingly chic in the simplest white shirt.

The white-on-white interior must be a layered look. When white is the common denominator, disparate design styles can comfortably coexist within one room. The drama comes from the tension between textures – rough with smooth, soft with hard, old with new. The key to the look is to experiment with unexpected combinations, mixing high-tech materials with antiques and junk. For example, juxtapose a pared-down modern table with a Louis Quinze chair and a Venetian glass triptych mirror. Humble pieces of junk furniture can be revived and transformed by a coat of white eggshell paint. An old-fashioned wooden trestle or wallpapering table can be smartened up with paint or covered with fabric.

Glass, translucent silk organza and sheer Perspex furniture add the subtle dream-like quality that is essential for an ice palace. The ice queen's favourite place to meditate is the Bubble chair, a see-through hanging Perspex seat that floats in space, designed by Eero Aarnio in 1968.

Touches of silver are the only permitted distraction from whiteness and translucency. A giant screen-printed silver feather (see page 18) works both as a room divider and an effective alternative to a painting. A mirror, together with flashes of silver leaf on a picture frame or screen, reflects and energizes the room's light.

get the look

walls

Start with the perfect blank canvas that maximizes the sense of light and space. Walls may have to be painted and repainted in the never-ending quest for the ultimate shade of white – neither too dazzling nor too 'dirty'. Off-white is much more forgiving than brilliant white; its impact is softer and it doesn't show marks as easily. If walls need to be replastered, try raw white plaster left unpainted and finished with an application of wax. To add drama, apply silver leaf or metallic water-based paint to a single wall or a door. Alternatively, cover a large artist's canvas in silver leaf and display it like a painting. Fake a mirror by applying silver leaf in a square or rectangle to one section of a wall, such as above a fireplace or somewhere you might naturally hang a mirror.

Uneven walls benefit from a subtle paint effect. A 'linen' look can be achieved by using two whites, one lighter and one darker. Paint on one shade first, then mix the second shade with glaze and dry brush horizontally and vertically.

floors

Wooden floorboards can be bleached, limed or painted in gloss or matt paint, while some wood laminate floors come in very pale, almost-white shades. Achieve a seamless look by laying a floor made up of large squares of plywood and paint these the same colour as the walls. Polished concrete is another 'hard' flooring option that looks appropriately sleek, as does plain white rubber. White carpet is rather impractical, so opt for Mongolian bleached lambskins or washable cotton woven runners to soften a hard floor. Shaggy cotton bath mats sewn together make an improvised tactile rug.

soft furnishings

Inexpensive utility fabrics like muslin or canvas look wonderful teamed with more decorative lace or silk. Snow camouflage fabric slung over a curtain pole makes an original modern alternative to lace. No-sew curtains can be made using new or antique sheets, or decorative tablecloths, held in place by curtain clips. Try a two-layer window treatment: flimsy organza panels to diffuse the light combined with heavy white velvet

drapes to obscure it. Hang fabrics from clear Perspex rods supported at the ends by simple chrome cup hooks.

Crisp white linen or canvas loose covers revamp upholstered furniture in an instant and can be easily washed. The lazy but stylish option is to wrap a soft white throw over a chair or sofa and secure it with a knot. Stiff organdie slipcovers look sexy on strict little chairs – the furnishing equivalent of a sheer shirt over a pretty bra.

For the ultimate romantic place to sleep, make a sheer or semi-sheer canopy or tent that drapes over the bed to give the sense of a secret space within a space, or hang petticoats, dresses and slips around the framework of a canopy bed.

lights

Decorative chandeliers with clear glass or Perspex drops are ideal for lighting an ice palace. An artfully twisted tree branch painted white and wrapped with a strand of white electric fairy lights makes a magical alternative. Another inexpensive substitute that also has an ethereal effect is a group of several long, floaty organza or paper shades hung together. Tall table lamps with delicately spun resin shades, adorned with flimsy strands of feather, create pools of soft light. Plain white cotton or paper shades can be embellished with mother-of-pearl buttons, opalescent sequins, leaf skeletons or feathers.

how to

1. To make a canopy above a bed, attach four cup hooks to the ceiling above the four corners of the bed.

2. Suspend two Perspex rods from the hooks with fishing wire.

3. Drape some filmy fabric like organza, net or muslin over the rods.

• **Variation:** An antique corona fixed to the wall above the head of the bed is the natural alternative to a canopy and dresses up a simple divan. Attach some light, gauzy fabric to the two halves of the semicircle so that the fabric falls away to each side of the bed.

intage girl

An old-fashioned girl is a 'second-hand Rose', as the song says.
She can't be bothered with newfangled minimalism or anything too sleek and shiny; her tastes are more 'down home'. You'll find her drooling over Ralph Lauren adverts in glossy magazines, watching *The Waltons* on television, reading Louisa May Allcott books, baking cakes in the kitchen, and making patchwork quilts. Her style is a fusion of England and New England, and her boudoir is a nostalgic attic eyrie in which she takes refuge from the onslaught of the innovative and overdesigned twenty-first century.

The vintage girl knows just how to mix and match florals, stripes, checks and spots. She would never dream of substituting blankets and sheets for a duvet and loathes the idea of everything matching. A natural hoarder, she scours jumble sales for hand-knitted blankets, second-hand brushed-cotton sheets, old enamel jugs or chintz curtains. The vintage girl has a rather 'make-do and mend' attitude to design; she enjoys the idea that she is recycling, cherishing faded, torn, much-loved junk and jumble and injecting it with new life. She keeps a jar of buttons, a tangle of ribbons and ricrac braid, balls of wool and patchwork pieces in her capacious tapestry sewing bag, ever ready to customize a new find.

She dreams of owning a white New England clapboard cottage, complete with a swing on the verandah, where she could spend long afternoons sipping home-made lemonade, and reading cookery books. Unashamedly feminine, she celebrates old-fashioned skills like embroidery and jam-making. Weekends are devoted to honing her home-making skills and trawling church bazaars for bargains. Travel in her wake and you will be enveloped in the scent of cinnamon, buttered toast and beeswax polish.

style signature

The vintage girl can't keep away from junk shops, vintage-clothes shops and auctions. She simply would not countenance introducing anything new into her temple of 'shabby chic'. Nothing pleases her more than finding an enamel-topped kitchen table with peeling layers of paint, or an old kitchen chair shedding a layer of shoddily applied gloss to reveal a jaunty colour underneath. She has a knack for inventing new uses for old furniture: an old metal school locker becomes a wardrobe; wooden vegetable crates become storage units for scraps of fabric and blankets. A collection of mismatched rosy china cups is infinitely more charming than a conventional tea set. The vintage girl never throws anything away. Scraps of leftover rose-print wallpaper are used to cover books and storage boxes or to line the insides of drawers and cupboards. Ageing jumpers are divested of their sleeves and turned into cosy covers for cushions or hot-water bottles. Even her ironing board and clothes' hangers are covered in floral-print fabric. Fraying edges are bound with contrasting ribbon and holes are darned or patched.

The danger is that the whole thing could become madly busy and 'grannyish', but the vintage girl avoids this by balancing pattern with plenty of white paint on the walls and furniture. This gives the whole look a freshness that is usually lacking in 'country style' decorating.

'mix and match' and 'waste not, want not' apply to everything

'The roses were in flower ... cabbage roses on thick stalks, moss roses, always in bud, pink smooth beauties opening curl on curl ...'

Katherine Mansfield, *Prelude*

get the look

walls

A blank, white shell makes a good starting point. Character can be added with tongue-and-groove or panelled walls – think Suffolk beach hut or Martha's Vineyard clapboard. Tongue-and-groove is available at any good do-it-yourself or hardware store, while panelling can be faked by attaching a grid of fibreboard strips, 5 cm (2 in) wide, onto a plain wall and painting it all one colour.

Wallpaper does not have to wrap around the whole room. Try papering just one wall, perhaps behind the bed, or use lavish rose-print paper on a folding screen. If you are bored by an all-white room, pull a colour scheme together by painting skirting boards (baseboards), doors and picture rails in a subtle colour (if you have a favourite piece of painted furniture, copy the shade).

floors

Revamp old floorboards with hard-wearing floor paint; a chequerboard effect or broad stripes in contrasting colours look suitably homespun. Pick two soft colours from the general scheme: apple green and cream looks fresh with florals, and a pale grey with off-white is classic. For comfort, add rag rugs, faded floral rugs or Scandinavian cotton runners.

furniture

Coats of white eggshell paint will instantly revive junk furniture and sometimes it is worth scratching the existing surface to see if there is a more exciting colour underneath. Leaving wooden tables and chairs out in the garden is a lazy way to achieve a distressed look, but peeling paintwork should be sealed with a yacht varnish.

Simple garden furniture looks at home indoors, too. Hunt down slatted wooden and metal folding chairs, slatted tables and folding metal café tables. A trestle table makes a utilitarian dressing table or desk. Pretty it up by painting the top or covering it with floral or gingham oilcloth. Customize a plain chest of drawers by covering the entire piece in fabric or by neatly gluing on strips of braid or ribbon. Revamp a chair with a crisp slipcover made from linen tea towels or another utility fabric, such as canvas. Display decorative accessories – anything from handbags and hats to dresses and beads – on a long wooden peg rail. Vintage girls love traditional cast-iron brass or enamel-framed beds, or romantic French daybeds. A daybed is practical in a small space as it can double up as a sofa. Just cover the mattress with a cosy blanket and scatter it with pillows during the day. An old metal washstand with a matching jug is another anachronistic but charming addition to the vintage boudoir. Fill the jug with untamed wild flowers and keep jam jars full of small posies.

soft furnishings

You can be really inventive with second-hand textiles. An old wing chair looks cosy reupholstered in a blanket (if one blanket will not cover the entire chair, use two different ones).

Fringed blankets hung from old wooden rings make charming winter curtains. Alternatively, buy brushed-cotton pyjama-striped fabric for highly original lightweight curtains, while lacy or cutwork cloths make ideal summer drapes. Turn old curtains into quilts, cushion covers or tablecloths. You can even frame a particularly painterly piece of fabric and hang it as a picture. Plain bed linen can be jazzed up with basic embroidery – blanket-stitch edges or chain-stitch words and monograms – or use gingham ribbons, ricrac braid and old dress fabric as a contrasting trim. Get your knitting needles out and make a throw that coordinates with the bed linen from 24-cm (10-inch) squares stitched together.

lights

Mix different styles together – from utilitarian metal shades on angle-poise lamps to fairy lights or tea lights in jam jars. Floral enamel chandeliers look better than the French crystal-drop kind.

how to

The most innovative thing to do with all those chipped china plates, odd tiles and broken cups that you cannot bear to part with is to smash them into a thousand mosaic pieces and create a tabletop (see left).

1. Prepare a simple metal or wood tabletop with tile adhesive, texturing it with wavy lines using stiff card.

2. Arrange the multicoloured china pieces into an attractive design on the surface.

3. Cover the pieces with tile grout, making sure you fill in all the cracks. Wipe over the whole surface with a damp cloth to get rid of excess grout before it sets.

• **Variation:** China mosaics can also brighten up terracotta plant pots, vases, jugs and picture frames.

• **Variation:** Experiment with colour and pattern. Mix different shades of white china or simply use patterned blue and white on a surface.

Boho

The boho girl is a broad-minded free spirit who loves to live
surrounded by exquisite and exotic things from the past, from her friends and family, or
collected on her travels. A dedicated maximalist, she would never 'pare down' or rationalize
her possessions. Disdaining fashion, she lives a bolder, broader life than her style-obsessed
sisters. 'This season' means absolutely nothing to her; it goes against the grain to pay attention
to puerile fashion diktats. With her ankle-length petticoats, arms engulfed in ethnic bangles
and ancient frock coat, she has always dressed like a contemporary version of Frieda Kahlo
and resents the fact that the fashionistas have adopted her fancy-dress look as their own.

The boho girl loves character, patina and history. The objects she acquires have their
own stories – anecdotes that she tells again and again to curious admirers. Faded, ripped and
torn, she overlooks their faults and sees only ravished beauty. Her cats have taken up residence
on a Georgian wing-chair that is spilling horsehair stuffing and covered in shredded silk damask.
Logic does not seem to apply. There is no earthly reason why someone should keep a collection
of silver teapots in the bathroom, but it looks charming and she has to put it somewhere.

Her rooms may be tumbledown, draughty, cramped, disorganized even, but they will always
be charming. She has a knack for throwing the oddest ingredients into the pot and making
something deliciously individual. Everything she does is suffused with artless, effortless *joie
de vivre*. The flowers that she buys are not arranged but unceremoniously plonked in a jug.
A jumble of assorted footwear – from beaded slippers to Spanish goatherd's boots – gathers
dust beneath the bed. Her rugs are threadbare, her linen crumpled, but somehow none of
this matters. It is all utterly enchanting.

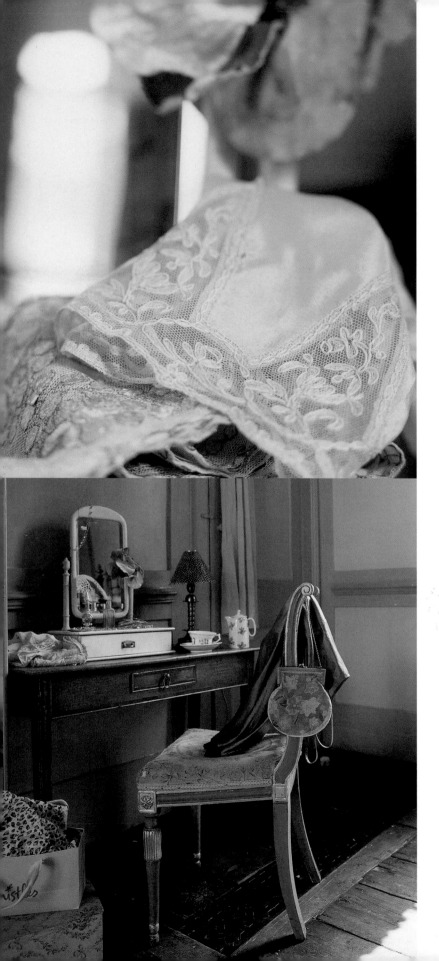

style signature

The boho boudoir is all about a reverence for history and a thirst for the exotic. There is a complete lack of artifice and a disregard for current decorating idioms. Rooms are furnished with pieces inherited from a venerable relative or acquired rather haphazardly with no idea of 'coordination'. A family portrait or a watercolour by a favourite aunt hangs next to tribal masks from far-flung journeys. The boho girl haunts auctions, rifles skips and borrows from friends. The worn silk curtains remind her of childhood holidays in Norfolk. Her matchless Irish linen sheets and bias-cut evening dresses were part of Granny's wedding trousseau. Among all the rickety junk are a number of really good pieces: the hand-painted eighteenth-century French chair at the dressing table; the painted cast-iron bed; a *Directoire* chaise longue.

The boho girl adores lamps with amusing little shades made of feathers or ruched chiffon. Although she had no particular colour scheme in mind, she is drawn to raspberry reds and papal purples, as they complement her pale complexion. As her closets are stuffed to the gills, she keeps current outfits draped about the room. She has a 'linen press' of sorts, where she hoards garish crocheted throws, blankets, embroidered hand towels and cosmetics from her apothecary. She loves to display.

The boho girl is the only one who can get away with scuffed shoes, unironed shirts and uncombed hair, yet still manage to look completely ravishing and original. Her home imitates her sartorial style and is always in a state of charming dishevelment and disarray. Introduce anything really smart or overdesigned and the whole balance is thrown horribly. It would never occur to her to visit Ikea for a flat-packed wardrobe when there is a local street market, auction house and junk emporium around the corner. Nor would a dishwasher, microwave, tea bags or jar of instant coffee ever appear on the boho girl's shopping list. She has her standards.

get the look

walls

For examples of wall decoration, think of an artist's attic. Use muted colours in sage greens, tobacco browns or steely blues. Two shades of one colour work well on panels, or above and below picture or dado rails. Panelled or tongue-and-groove walls are more characterful than plain. If the 'newly painted' effect is too slick, distress walls with wire wool or antiquing patina.

Rubbed-back plaster also looks good with antiques. Add whiting or chalk powder to water-based paint then apply two or three separate coats of paint in different, but related, colours. Rub back the walls with sandpaper in order to reveal the previous layers in places.

Many a boho decorator has painstakingly peeled off ancient layers of wallpaper to discover delightfully 'distressed' walls beneath. If you want to preserve artfully mottled, chalky surfaces, seal them with a flat, matt varnish.

furniture

Explaining how to do boho is like describing how to be sexy. No-one can tell you how to be eccentric, but if you follow

your heart you will inevitably 'get the look'. Mix a few pieces of 'serious' furniture with anything that takes your fancy. An eclectic mix works surprisingly well when it has been chosen by the same person. For inspiration, visit stately homes in England, particularly the home of the Bloomsbury Group in Charleston, East Sussex, where every surface and stick of furniture has been decorated with paint. The result is a very individual look that is influenced by fine art but is also personal and cosy. For a similar 'shabby chic' appearance, sandblast furniture to age and distress it. A basic divan can be turned into an opulent daybed by covering it with a lavish dark velvet throw and adding a long bolster and extravagantly covered scatter cushions in rich colours and different textures.

soft furnishings

Clever recycling is the key to the boho approach to textiles. Cover a well-worn chaise longue with a patchwork throw made up of scraps of worn-out dresses and damask fragments from old curtains. Search for faded, second-hand curtains, which can be hung as they are or altered to fit your windows. Tapestries, linen sheets and wool blankets can all be used to make unusual window treatments.

accessories

Break all the rules – let nothing match and never buy pairs of anything; indulge your passions. One dedicated boho decorator has a collection of white jugs in every conceivable shape or size, which live on top of an armoire in her bedroom. Another has a glass-fronted cabinet crammed full of ephemera from travels in South America – everything from paper garlands to costume dolls. It is unusual to come across a boho girl who has actually finished decorating her home. The whole point of the style, or anti-style, is that it is a work in progress. There will always be surfaces to decorate and newly found objects to incorporate.

'With the exception of the four-poster ... all the good furniture has been sold and replaced by minimum requirements bought in junk-shops ... I keep my bedside candle on a battered tin trunk that cost one shilling; Rose keeps hers on a chest of drawers painted to imitate marble, but looking more like bacon.'

Dodie Smith, *I Capture the Castle*
(Smith's heroine, Cassandra, and her sister Rose live the ultimate bohemian life in a freezing-cold, tumbledown castle.)

how to

• Upholster a chair or sofa in the boho style. Forget all about coordinating swatches and trim. Instead, copy David Hockney's beach-house chairs and fling together a selection of wildly patterned textiles. Get your upholsterer to cover every section – arms, back, seat and sides – in a different fabric, mismatching checks, florals and stripes.

• Loose covers hide less-than-perfect shapes and are an easy way to change the mood of a room from winter to summer. Use inexpensive tickings, combining different widths of stripe, to achieve a fresh look.

Dangerous liaisons

A romantic, a dreamer, an intellectual and, most importantly, a Francophile, the dangerous liaisons girl feels compelled to capture the grandeur and opulence of the past and contrives a boudoir that is dedicated to French eighteenth- and nineteenth-century style. In a former life, 'la châtelaine' (the hostess) was probably a mistress of Le Roi Soleil (that's Louis XIV to you and me). She peppers every sentence with some aphorism of Racine's in her immaculate French accent, and is forever dropping a copy of Baudelaire's *Les fleurs du mal* onto your coffee table. Unashamedly feminine, she delights in the ornate curves of nineteenth-century fauteuil chairs, the romance of fading toile de Jouy, gilded mirrors and Empire *chaises*. She cannot fail to feel as powerful as Laclos's Marquise in this theatrical setting.

While her heroine Marie Antoinette amused herself by playing at being a shepherdess, la châtelaine pretends to be a pre-revolutionary aristocrat (*A Tale of Two Cities* is her favourite book). She fancies herself as a *précieuse*, one of the sophisticates who instigated the salons and gatherings of artists and poets. There is something at once comforting and forbidding about the throne-like chairs and crumbling gilt. The elegant decay of rickety bergère chairs and peeling paint is an essential part of 'faded grandeur'. Besides, it's all horribly bourgeois to be surrounded by perfect antiques. La châtelaine indulges her 'gilt trip' in all her possessions, but this is toned down by ragged silk edges and lumpen upholstery.

style signature

Simulating the proportions, grandeur and ambience of a traditional French château in a less than palatial room presents the Francophile with obvious problems. Real eighteenth-century French rooms were elegant, but rather spare, with furniture such as marble-topped consoles and gilt chairs usually kept in a strict, ordered fashion against the walls. The other clear advantage that these rooms had over their modern-day counterparts is interesting architectural details – mouldings, catches, handles, doors, windows with shutters and herringbone parquet flooring. The solution is to fake it: install shutters and a reclaimed wooden parquet floor, and change door handles and plaster mouldings.

'Whoever does not visit Paris regularly will never really be elegant.'

Honoré de Balzac

The Francophile will travel any distance to indulge her passion for *l'art de vivre français*. She knows that the best bargains are to be found in France at *dépôt-ventes* (warehouses crammed with bargins) and *les marches aux puces* (flea markets). While motoring through the sleepy backwaters she screeches to a halt every time she sees a *brocante* sign. This is lifestyle shopping, where the pursuit of the bargain is as pleasurable to the shopper as the resulting purchase. And it is addictive.

The dangerous liaisons girl is not a purist and is apt to mix pieces from different periods and sources. Her bed is dressed with aubergine toile de Jouy and her screen is covered in rose madder toile. Her low table is a painted, metal, 1950s junk-shop find and her chest of drawers is an Eastern-influenced bamboo piece. The large decorative grey-painted armoire in her dressing room was an investment which, she felt, 'belonged' with the dressing table she already owned. It incorporates a full-length mirror and two large sections of hanging space. The muted scheme includes a pair of fauteuil chairs, upholstered in grape satin-finish cotton. The whole effect of the room is restful, making her daily 'toilette' an enjoyable ritual.

get the look

walls

White and gold are the colours of the French eighteenth century. Châteaux walls were white and panelled with touches of gilt. But you can fake the look by applying sketchy gilt faux panels to plain walls and treat your room as a stage set. French decorator Frédéric Méchiche is the master of this style. If the apartments he decorates are not already panelled, he adds fake architectural detail with tall screens painted with swags and tails.

floors

The floors of elegant Parisian apartments are often laid with herringbone parquet. Find and fit reclaimed floors, which have more character than new versions, and accessorize them with Aubusson rugs, the subtly coloured tapestries that became very popular during the reign of Louis XIV.

furniture and accessories

Design writer Herbert Ypma identifies the Gallic talent for putting together things from different centuries, naming the French 'indefatigable foragers'. Their homes demonstrate a love of *objets trouvés*, and sometimes they mix together the humblest of objects with serious antiques to achieve quixotic, imaginative interior schemes.

With so many antique dealers in love with the French look, finding the right furniture is very straightforward. Both the Parisian *marche aux puces* and the huge antique and *brocante* fairs held in Lille in France are fabulous hunting grounds where you may still pick up bargains. A French publication called *Aladdin* informs enthusiasts about the dates and whereabouts of such fairs. For chairs, think in pairs: place two gilded and caned bergère or two fauteuil chairs (upholstered and with arms) against a wall on either side of a marble-topped console. Light up your boudoir with intricate wall sconces (electric or candlelit), chandeliers and candlesticks. Balance formality with informality.

soft furnishings

Toile de Jouy, a cotton fabric depicting everyday scenes of life in the eighteenth century, came from the eponymous town of Jouy, close to Versailles in France. It is still possible to find good antique pieces, but there are also many contemporary imitations (for example, the quilted toile pillows and bed cover pictured on pages 46–7).

Generally, toile is produced in four colours: rose madder, aubergine, indigo and grey. A room completely filled with toile de Jouy in one hue can look wonderful: a pastoral world of its own. Alternatively, for a more relaxed look, combine toile with other fabrics, such as striped mattress ticking in a matching shade (red toile with red ticking, for example). Use fabric en masse on the walls, to make a bed canopy or for upholstery, cushions and curtains. If this look is too busy for you, invest in a single antique piece of fabric and restrict its use to a simple screen or small chair.

hunting for bargains in France

Friperie
If you want to find antique bed or table linen, head for the local friperie, a warehouse full of tempting textiles. Consult the local tourist office about where to find these goldmines.

Les Puces
Parisian flea markets, full of all sorts of treasures, are held at G Brassens Square, Porte de Montreuil and St Ouen. Be prepared to rise early (7.30 am) to find the best bargains.

Brocantes
Big brocante fairs are three- or four-day events that are held annually or biannually all over France. Lille is acknowledged to be one of the best.

Dépôt-ventes or Greniers
Every town has one of these warehouses, packed full of furniture, bathroom accessories, linen, and so on.

sexy

Urban playgirl

The urban playgirl's life is one long party. It is what she does best:
she's a professional. It is no accident that her boudoir is a clone of her favourite nightclub – she designed it that way. After a fun-packed round of gallery opening, magazine launch, dinner and late cocktails, followed by dancing, she and her posse of other playgirls can always retire to her place to chill out, and barely realize that they have moved on from the last venue.

Her urban loft is a mere stone's throw from the action. A dedicated city girl, she has no intention of retiring to leafy suburban Stepford territory. Never. Too much green space makes her nervous. Fresh air makes her tired. Silence makes her want to scream. She can only rest if she is guaranteed the possibility of non-stop 24-hour distraction on her doorstep – espresso bars, all-night delis, secret drinking dens, private members' clubs. Her Gucci wallet bulges with membership cards. She circumvents the door whore's vetting procedure and sweeps straight through to the VIP lounge within the blink of a false eyelash.

As she can't boil an egg, she decided that a kitchen is surplus to requirements. She turned the larger portion of her apartment into a bedroom-cum-sunken lounging area, and there is plenty of space for dancing. Recovery pyjama parties are long, drawn-out affairs, sometimes stretching into the next evening, when, at about 6 pm, playgirls remove their satin sleep masks and start the preparation ritual all over again.

style signature

It all started with the purple padded wall behind her bed. She intended to construct a padded headboard, but it suddenly seemed more decadent to cover the whole wall in velvet squares and the opposite wall in silver leaf. The bed is her sanctuary, her workstation, her throne. If she ever sees daylight, she spends her time on the phone, herding up her compatriots and inviting the right people to the week's events. Slinking into the night in a barely-there dress and vertiginous heels, she looks forward to the moment when she can slip once again between silk-satin sheets and, with the touch of a remote control, switch on MTV. Of course, the television is cleverly hidden behind a vast expanse of purple velvet drapes.

'seize
the night'

the urban playgirl's mantra

Urban playpens have little to do with normal homes. They run in a different time zone and their priorities are set accordingly. A professional playgirl is bound to have an enormous fridge-freezer, full of champagne, vodka and Bloody Mary mix.

She enjoys futuristic 1970s design, especially space-age shapes in Perspex or white fibreglass. She likes to play *Barbarella*. Sunken lounges, 'conversation pits', hanging ball chairs, psychedelic colours and any of the adventurous innovations explored by designers like Alberto Pinto from the 1960s onwards attract her.

get the look

furniture

An eclectic mixture of kitsch theatrical pieces – like tarty little French chairs, 1950s cocktail bars or curvaceous repro velvet sofas – and classic, mid-twentieth-century furniture comprises the clubby look. Scandinavian designers Eero Saarinen and Verner Panton produced sculptural shapes that have become design classics and key pieces. The white fibreglass Tulip chairs and tables and the Panton, the first single-material, single-form, injection-moulded chair, are still available from specialist vintage shops or as brand-new reproductions.

floors

Polished concrete or seamless coloured resin are the ideal flooring options. Softer choices include shag-pile carpet (very 1970s lounge), pony-print cowhide or dyed long-haired lambskin.

walls

Take inspiration from your favourite restaurant, nightclub or hotel. Ian Schrager's new London hotel, The Sanderson, has entire walls and windows dreamily lined in gauzy white drapes hung from chrome curtain poles that stretch from one wall to another. To increase the sense of intimacy, windows are fitted with white Venetian blinds.

lights

Go for drama by choosing elaborate chandeliers and futuristic pendant and standard lights that resemble flying saucers. Oversized engraved brass lamps add a touch of exoticism and are perfect in such a large space. No urban playpen would be complete without a glitterball, preferably a revolving one and spot-lit for boogie nights in.

windows

Designer Ella Doran makes the ideal window treatment for the urban playgirl's loft. Her roller blinds are printed with photographic images of neon-lit Soho streets or city skylines. For 1970s kitsch, hang a ready-made beaded curtain of plastic jewels, or string together Perspex shapes (try 15-cm [6-in] rectangles with holes drilled through them at the top and bottom).

how to

Interior designer Shaun Clarkson used six different shades of yellow for his padded wall. But try a violet version, as above, or a multicoloured wall if the mood takes you.

1. Decide how many 30-cm (12-in) hardboard squares are needed to cover the wall and cut them out to fit.

2. Use a glue gun to attach foam, 2.5 cm (1 in) thick, to the front of each square panel.

3. Cover each panel with cotton velvet, using a staple gun to secure the fabric onto the back of the panels.

4. Attach each square individually to the wall with Velcro strips. To change the colour scheme, simply make another set of squares using fabric in different colours and, when it gets dusty, vacuum the wall.

5. To finish, hang a curtain over the opposite wall for a theatrical touch that also hides the 'engine room' – the playgirl's extensive wardrobe, television, stereo, and book and magazine collection.

• Variation: Build your wall as a room divider (a floor-to-ceiling double-sided box with a hollow interior). Use the velvet panels to conceal hidey-holes containing bedside paraphernalia.

Sensual modernist

Essentially a sybarite with a highly developed need for luxury, the sensual modernist wants to inhabit rooms that look and feel like hotel suites that cater to every sensual need or whim. When she flies, she takes a lavender-scented pillow and a pashmina, just like her High Priestess, Donna Karan. Her rooms are heady with amber-scented designer candles; her hot-water bottle is snugly encased in a padded velvet or cashmere cover; she drinks proper tea made from tea leaves out of bone china cups; and she is never happier than when attired in loose pyjamas. Given the chance, she would run her whole life from an immaculately appointed 'power den', tapping softly on an ergonomically designed laptop in a colour that coordinates with her oh-so-subtle decorating scheme.

No mere label addict, she worships *le grand luxe*. The words 'bespoke' and 'handmade' send appreciative shivers down her well-aligned spine. The sensual modernist was the kind of teenager who saved her pocket money for weeks to buy cashmere socks. At thirteen she held forth about the merits of handmade brogues and tailored suits, and she has always sported a rarely stocked brand of jeans, only available in Paris.

A master of subtlety, she has invested in a state-of-the-art flat-screen television and a discreet silver CD player, which does not jar with the nude suede walls and wenge-wood consoles. Look inside her wardrobe and you will find row upon row of sombre, almost-identical garments made of rare and exquisite fabrics. She often finds it difficult to leave her home, as other environments rarely meet her elevated standards.

style signature

The sensual modernist's knack is to create a look that is international, über-sophisticated and even pared-down, but never cold and soulless. She delights in texture. Linen must be Egyptian cotton; blankets the softest merino wool or cashmere or polar fleece; and pillows the lightest Siberian goosedown. Soothing neutral colours are easier on the eye than brights, so she opts for creams, chocolates, greys and taupes, sometimes accented by sage green or celadon blue. Choosing different shades of the same colour is a very effective sensual-modernist approach to decorating, and she may combine, say, the palest grey silk with regulation grey flannel and anthracite grey velvet.

Her boudoir is a sanctuary from all the stress and shoddiness of the outside world. Here, every sense needs to be considered. Disciples of this school of thought burn mood-enhancing essential oils, scented candles or incense and tread softly on sheepskin, leather floor tiles or thick, deep-pile wool carpets. Sofas and daybeds are heaped with cosy throws and cushions in butter-soft suede and leather that smells as good as it feels to the skin.

'All **credibility,** all **good** conscience, all **evidence** of truth comes **only** from the **senses.**'

Friedrich Nietzsche

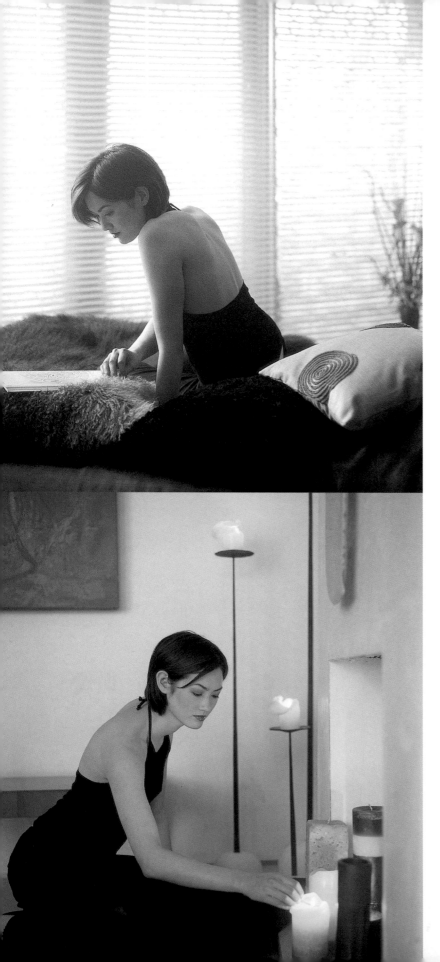

get the look

floors

The ultimate sensual-modernist floor must be leather – it is warm underfoot and ages beautifully. Other feel-good floorings include shaggy suede rugs, cosy felt carpets and cowhide.

furniture

Simple lines suit the sensual-modernist aesthetic. Furniture shapes may be modern, but are softened by soft, tactile textiles. Comfort is key. The sensual modernist is a real believer in buying well-made pieces that will not date. Here, a large suede square works both as low-level seating and a coffee table. The design classics that will 'last forever' include anything by Florence Knoll or Antonio Citterio. Large hotel-style beds are favoured. These can be assembled easily from a rectangle of fibreboard covered on one side with foam, 7.5 cm (3 in) thick, and then upholstered in a strong, sensual fabric such as Alcantara. The board can be bolted to the wall behind a divan bed. Complete the look with regimented piles of pillows and cushions and a tailored valance in a toning colour.

soft furnishings

The softest fabrics and colours are the basis for the sensual look. Leather, suede and sheepskin, cashmere and linen can be used in muted shades of nude, chocolate, taupe and khaki. Although the colour palette is deliberately limited, the range of textures is endless: moc-croc, alligator, snakeskin, washable fake suede and hides. Really indulgent curtains can be made from chamois leather or pashmina wool.

lights

Down light is provided by a bespoke lighting scheme – recessed halogen spots with dimmer switches – to ensure the right mood. Flickering candlelight is ultra-soothing. Large sculptural candles last for ages and groups of church candles create pools of warm light. Lamps with chunky, rectangular leather bases and suede shades are the perfect accessories.

'COCOON
and COCOON'

the sensual modernist mantra

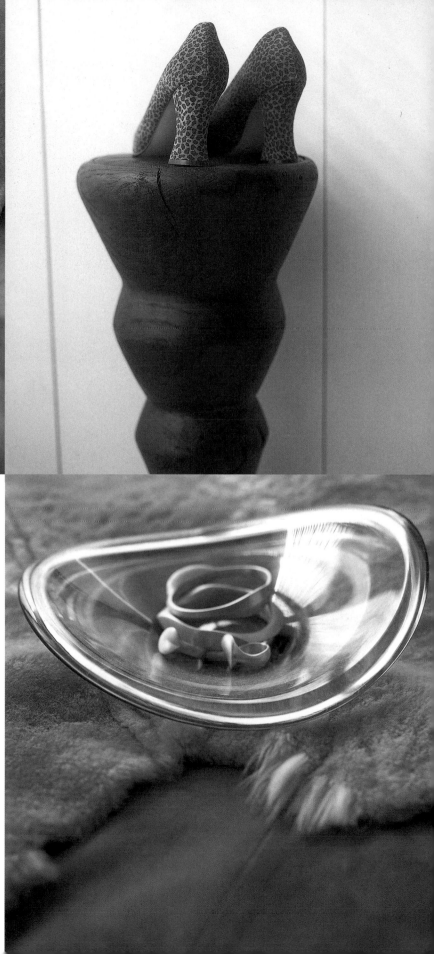

Indulge yourself
with aromas

Spice up your dreams
and your love life with
a potion composed of
pink or red rose petals
and a few vanilla pods,
sprinkled with essential
oils of frankincense and
sandalwood. Keep the
potpourri in a bowl or
fill a sachet and slip it
inside your pillowcase.
Alternatively, vaporize
the following blend
of essential oils in
an oil burner:

3 drops of rose
2 drops of jasmine
2 drops of lime
1 drop of cinnamon

Try out Culpeper's
recipe for scented
pink rosewater:
fill a saucepan with the
red petals of heavily
scented roses, add
water and bring to the
boil. Allow to cool with
the cover still in place
and, when cold, strain.
Spray onto linen while
ironing or spritz onto
towels and bed linen.

Fetishista

Be afraid! The fetishista wants you to know she's a bad girl. Her iniquitous den leaves you in no doubt. Her skin is pale, her hair black as coal, her mouth a scarlet gash and her slanted eyes smoky with yesterday's liner. She cultivates a devil-may-care style that is not for the faint-hearted. Her boudoir is a fantasy realized, full of lip-gloss shiny, touchy-feely surfaces and cartoon-shaped furniture. The fetishista lives in an unhealthy perpetual darkness, the murky nightclub gloom of her boudoir lit by coloured neon tubes.

A giant spike-heeled stiletto, an erotic symbol of female dominance, was the beginning of her vision for the room. No comforting feminine fluffiness for her. She prefers to evoke the feminine with undulating curves and provocative imagery. Cult illustrator Alan Jones's voluptuous dominatrices are her role models. These scantily clad supervixens have the same arched eyebrows and wasp waists. The fetishista is a maverick with a degree in breaking rules. She is the sort of girl your mother warned you to stay away from: known for her petulant, iconoclastic behaviour, for defacing school property and improperly customizing her school uniform. Her carefully constructed persona simultaneously warns you to stay away and tempts you in. Similarly, her room is paradoxically both hard and soft.

style signature

The Alan Jones's stiletto screen inspired a primary colour combination of cobalt blue, jet black and white, to which the fetishista adds her trademark lipstick red. The slick, shiny wet-look PVC Archizoom modular Superonda sofa, designed in the future-obsessed 1960s, works as both sofa and divan.

The fetishista reveres the ground-breaking designers of the 1960s. Rather than functional seating, she covets the Tangeri bed, a sumptuous red velvet sofabed designed by Francesco Binfare for Edra, or a Pantower, Vernon Panton's mutilevel, fabric-covered, foam-upholstered frame, described as an 'apparatus for interactive play'. She owns other Panton classics, such as the Panton, a streamlined injection-moulded chair in futuristic white, and his Fountain chair, a lightweight plastic form that can work as both table and chair. It looks like a three-dimensional pool of water when lying on its long side, but is a contorted, sculptural 'S' shape when upright. All of these pieces are flexible, hard-wearing classics that come in the right bright primary colours.

The fetishista has put together a zoo of snazzy textural cushions, combining snakeskin, moc-croc and moc-alligator, scarlet cowhide and pearlized snakeskin-print leather. Her floors are decked out in animal-skin rugs, beneath which is her favourite material of all – rubber.

'I'm not bad, I was just drawn that way.'

Jessica Rabbit,
Who Framed Roger Rabbit

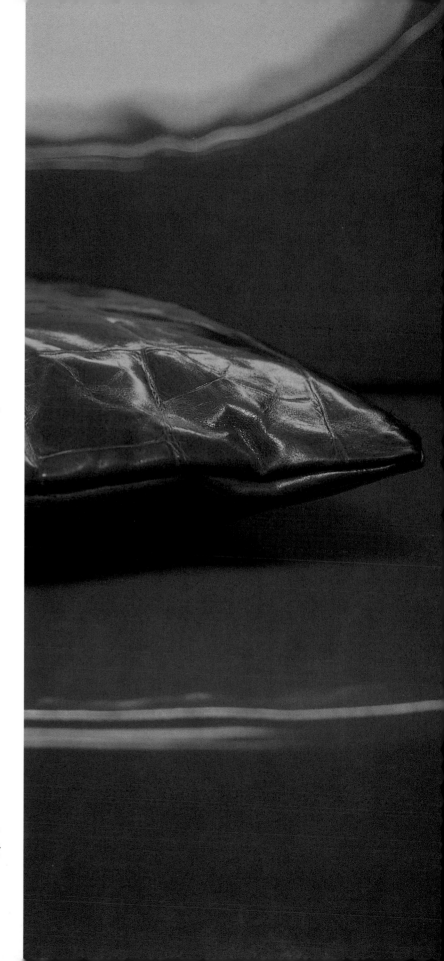

get the look

walls

The supervixen wallpaper by Alan Jones (see below) was cut up, framed and hung as a series of pictures, rather than pasted straight onto the walls. The same wallpaper would also create an impact when used on a screen or on cupboard doors. Daring decorating options include shiny PVC, available on rolls, fake suede and snakeskin-print wallpaper. Outlandish materials can often be tracked down through businesses that specialize in retail display. Alternatively, try metallic or glitter paints in snazzy colours.

floors

The obvious choice has to be rubber, but this type of flooring requires extreme care with stiletto heels. Soften the surface with sensual shaggy lambskin rugs.

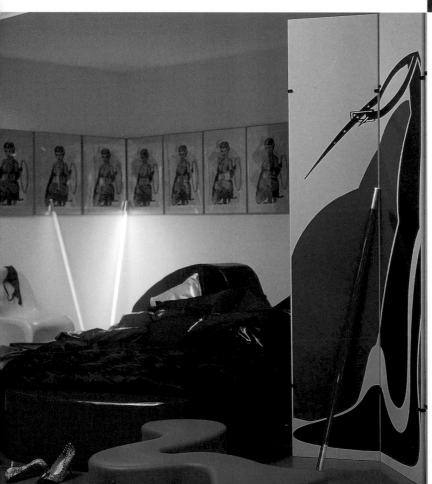

furniture

Futuristic shapes give the boudoir a surreal edge. All of the pieces pictured here were designed in the 1960s, so search the shops and websites that deal in furniture from this time period. Many designs are still manufactured today because they look as fresh and new now as they did at the time of their conception. Use low-level pieces that will help create an informal lounge look.

For storage, trawl junk shops for 'G' plan-style sideboards, tables and chests of drawers in streamlined 1950s shapes with spiky feet. Cheap and nasty ginger-brown mahogany is a no-no, but these unpromising pieces can be simply and stylishly transformed with coats of black gloss paint, spray-painted for a perfect finish or covered in snakeskin wallpaper.

soft/hard furnishings

As daylight is rarely a requirement in the fetishista's 'twilight zone', install blackout blinds and have fun with rubber or

'Every rococo **desire** the **mind** of man might, **in its perverse** ingenuity, devise found **ample** gratification here …'

Angela Carter, *The Loves of Lady Purple*

PVC curtains (punch holes in the headings and finish with metal eyelets). Tint window panes with adhesive stained-glass film or alternatively, track down photographic gels. Printed or embossed wet-look PVC, mixed with vinyl or leather, can be used to create a range of strokeable cushions in different shapes and sizes. Personalize plain white surfaces, such as roller blinds, bed sheets and pillowcases, with photographic images at your local photo lab. Use a graphic image of voluptuous scarlet lips or take a photograph of some wicked heels.

lights

Coloured neon tube lights are the perfect solution, and cast a suitably sultry light. For a softer glow, invest in Tom Dixon's Jack lights. These giant plastic 'jack' shapes can be stacked and used as a stool as well as a light source. Photographer's lightboxes fixed to the wall would also fit in well stylistically with the mood of her den.

Fashionista

Astoundingly precocious, the fashionista graduated from *Jackie* to *Vogue* at a very early age. At eleven she could spot an Yves Saint Laurent 'Le Smoking' jacket at 20 paces and knew more about the goings-on at Fashion HQ than the most hardened Fleet Street hack. While her contemporaries fantasized about ponies and gymkhanas, she was planning a couture trousseau (a word gleaned from Nancy Mitford novels) to be bought in Paris. She just needed to meet the right prince – or get a lowly, badly paid position tidying up the fashion cupboard at a glossy magazine. The opportunity to stroke the rows of absurdly inaccessible designer duds makes her blissfully happy, as does the lure of future press discounts and the goody bags (grown-up 'going home presents') that her superiors coo over after lashings of free champagne and canapés.

Decorating a home presents the fashionista with an excruciating dilemma: how to live in a stylish, envy-inducing pad without sacrificing this season's must-have accessories. The inexorable frogmarch of fashion demands such financial dedication that the fledgling fashionista is hard-pressed to afford the most basic Ikea flat-pack. However, the inventive style maven devises a scheme that makes her precious booty the hero of the room. Her boudoir becomes a fashion theme park, a vehicle for displaying her style credentials. Clever vintage finds rub seams with the *dernier cri* in footwear, handbags and lingerie.

SCANDALE
GAINES · CEINTURES · SOUTIEN-GORGE

style signature

If a fashionista's boudoir ends up looking more like a shop than a bedroom, this is exactly as it should be. Retail temples being her element, she would love to take up permanent residence in her favourite boutique. All the shop fittings, glass display cabinets, mannequins and hat stands are ideal for showing off her most prized possessions. She requires a flattering floor-length cheval mirror and a screen for costume changes. A glass-fronted armoire contains the collected works of Lulu Guinness; in other words, a tiny jewel-like handbag for every occasion.

Walls are hung with framed magazine covers and extracts from her coveted limited-edition book, *The Best of Flair*, as well as framed silk scarves by Hermès and Pucci. She can't bear to shut all her lovely things away in cupboards and drawers so she works out a seasonally rotating display system. Come spring, for example, out trot all the delicate spaghetti-strap sandals and kitten-heel mules to line up under the dressing table.

Cecil Beaton's classic, stylish black and white fashion plates are an obvious source of inspiration for a dedicated follower of fashion. Hamish Bowles, fashion director of American *Vogue*, and ultimate fashionista, admits to having been influenced by the society photographer himself at an early age. After making a pilgrimage to Beaton's House in Redditch, England, when he was a child, Bowles was so thrilled with the eclectic contents that he later took on the sophisticate's style and made it his own. He describes his fanciful New York apartment as resembling 'rooms in which a once-elegant nonagenarian socialite, fallen on hard times, had been forced to cram the considerable detritus of her well-travelled life. Fez embroideries, coloured-glass lanterns, and naïve *verre eglonise* paintings all suggest swag brought back from Tangier, my habitual summer haunt.' The recipe for the fashionista look perfectly described.

get the look

walls and floors

Choose a neutral, wrapround shade that works as a foil to stronger colours. Grey is a smart choice as it looks good with all shades of pinks, mauves, blues and greens, and offers scope for changing the look next season. Think of these blank surfaces as expansive display areas and devise innovative ways to show off your prized possessions. Cover an entire wall with framed favourite magazine covers and fashion illustrations, and hang your collection of designer bags from hooks. Copy the floor of Lulu Guinness's London showroom by trapping a patchwork of vintage covers beneath a piece of hard-wearing glass or Perspex. Witty handbags and amusing hats can be displayed on hat stands, dressmaker's dummies or luggage racks.

furniture

Since the emergence of chain stores and the subsequent demise of all those genteel little haberdashers and outfitters, many wonderful old shop fittings can be found at auctions and in junk shops. Glass-fronted cabinets divided into compartments or old apothecary units comprised of row upon row of tiny drawers provide appropriate storage for trinkets. Spindly gilt fashion-show chairs, tailor's mirrors (like the one behind the bed, below left), and screens and hatboxes are obvious must-haves for all fashionistas.

soft furnishings

Silk scarves can become cushion covers or art for walls. Last season's remnants could also serve the same purpose if you are feeling sufficiently ruthless. Cushions are definitely the new black; they are an easy way to update a colour scheme and they emphasize your grasp of modern decorating. For inspiration, think of films like *Funny Face* or *My Fair Lady*. And every fashionista worth her *Vogue* subscription should look to such icons as Geoffrey Beane, Diana Vreeland, Hamish Bowles or Edith Sitwell.

accessories

Think extravagant gesso mirrors, white plaster columns and huge sweeps of swagged silk damask. Elaborate picture frames, tarted up with a coat of white water-based paint, jostle with kitsch shell and cherub vases spilling vivid blooms. A twirly wrought-iron standard lamp is plastered with floral hair clips, ribbons, evening purses and hung with a butterfly-print organza dress. Baubles and beads drip from a sculptural pair of hands, once used to display gloves.

remember the fashionista's mantra
'accessorize
or be damned!'

how to

Assembling a mood board is a clever way to concentrate your ideas.

1. Collect magazine tear sheets, samples of fabric and wallpapers, paint swatches, postcards of inspiring paintings, confectionery wrappers, handmade papers, pretty buttons, feather trims from hats – anything that sums up your very particular tastes.

2. Pin all the pieces to a board, experimenting with their juxtapositions.

3. Apply the ideas to room decoration. Leopardskin could translate into a rug or throw; black and white fashion illustrations could appear framed on the walls; or the green silk of a ballet shoe with a black and fuchsia ribbon might suggest colours for the bed.

4. Remember that paint companies can match colours exactly, so your walls could be the same shade as your Manolo Blahnik slingbacks.

Starlet

The starlet's life is a series of grand entrances and exits. She is never satisfied unless jaws drop or eyes narrow with envy. Her polished look defines high-maintenance glamour. Naturally, the lavish, luxurious boudoir is the nerve centre of her campaign for world seduction. This is where she plans her strategy and keeps her arsenal of cosmetic weapons. An endless stream of beauty professionals pass through on a daily basis to perform the massages, manicures, facials and pedicures that are all essential to her rigorous schedule.

From an early age the starlet modelled herself on the sirens of black-and-white movies: Rita Hayworth, Ava Gardner, Lauren Bacall. She sports pale, pale skin and scarlet lips. Never under- or inappropriately dressed, she has a top-to-toe look for every occasion. A repertoire of style icons guide her every sartorial move. On waking, she asks herself, 'Who am I today?' For a simple lunch with girlfriends or a chaste first date, Audrey Hepburn supplies inspiration, while a private view or opening might require the Gallic sophistication of Catherine Deneuve.

She has a proper grown-up girl's walk-in wardrobe, planned by a storage expert. All her shoes live in boxes (polaroids are stuck to the front) and her hangers are padded satin or moth-repelling cedarwood. The system is meticulously regimented; shirts hang with other shirts, dresses with dresses, jumpers are expertly folded around lavender-scented tissue paper. The starlet's dry-cleaner knows her by her first name and sends her orchids on her birthday.

Unashamedly, she admits to being a label addict. Don't buy her underwear unless it's La Perla and remember the power of seductive packaging. There is nothing quite as thrilling to her as that rustle of tissue paper when purchases are deftly wrapped and slipped into stiff little bags (she's very proud of her collection of designer bags).

style signature

The modern starlet has contrived her boudoir style from the sets of 1930s and 1940s films which convinced her of her destiny. Hollywood fell in love with the mirrored furniture designed in France during the Depression (wood was in short supply, so mirror was used as a glamorous alternative). The postwar 1940s design aesthetic demanded generous, curvaceous shapes and proportions – a natural reaction to austerity. Rounded Art Deco chairs, satin sheets, a padded velvet eiderdown and giant, silk-covered cushions complete the look. The little scarlet boudoir chair embodies all the starlet's favourite qualities: neatness and elegance offset by frivolity. Upholstery is expertly detailed. The oversized cushions are made from lustrous fabrics that are pleated, buttoned, ruched, embroidered and trimmed.

The starlet's colour scheme is a daring mixture of her favourite lipstick shades of scarlet and mauve. On the bed you will find seven shades of red, a smattering of crocus yellow and purple. She mixes luxurious textures with abundance and reflective surfaces maximize the impact of all her props. Ostrich feather fans, crystal perfume bottles and powder puffs litter her dressing table and posies of vivid cut flowers abound. Acutely aware of the sensual impact of her boudoir, she ensures that all surfaces are tactile. When she kicks off her stilettos, pampered toes sink into the white Mongolian lambskin rugs that are dotted around her bed.

Always capricious, the starlet treats her bedroom as a set, to be changed and updated according to her mood. To add a vibrant splash of colour, she flings a lavishly fringed and embroidered piano shawl over her bed or chair. 'Costume' changes take place behind a padded silk-upholstered screen, which she found in a thrift store and re-covered. The screen also serves as a useful noticeboard, where she pins up invitations to openings and premieres, or ideas for new outfits torn from magazines.

Such a high-maintenance lifestyle demands careful organization, so she invests in innovative storage. Clear Perspex cubbyholes and drawers house everything from eyeshadows to feather boas. One day you'll find her perfectly preserved shoe collection in a museum.

Fickle when it comes to beauty products, her glass bathroom shelves groan under the weight of lotions, potions, serums and endless scent bottles. Her mother passed on a particular weakness for Guerlain. The French perfume house's pretty flacons (Shalimar, Mitsouko, L'Heure Bleue) look divine on her immaculate dressing table, along with a real feather powder puff and a set of antique silver brushes.

Her cosy boudoir takes on elements of a grand drawing room with its fat armchairs, a buttoned banquette and a drinks cabinet. She wouldn't dream of relaxing in any other room and even receives guests here.

get the look

floors

Wall-to-wall wool carpet in cream, white or a pretty pastel shade would suit this boudoir well. Deep-pile shaggy wool carpets and rugs are experiencing a revival and fit in exactly with the starlet's self-indulgent design criteria. Super-soft long-haired Mongolian lambskins come in white, but they can be dyed any colour, as can flotaki rugs. They can also be stitched together to make a larger, unfitted carpet.

furniture

Seek inspiration from films of the 1930s and 1940s, when lavish interiors played a part in every production. Imagine a combination of eighteenth-century French grandeur with the glamour of Hollywood. Curvaceous Art Deco shapes sit surprisingly well with Louis Quinze-style fauteuil chairs, elaborately carved mirrors and gilded, marble-topped consoles.

Scale is important here. Studio sets could accommodate vast sofas and oversized lamps, giving a 'larger than life feel' to the room. It is quite appropriate that a starlet's boudoir should resemble a hotel suite. She is, after all, in love with *Le Grand Luxe*. Cheat cleverly and you can achieve this look on a modest budget. Neglected Art Deco furniture is often available from junk stores and local auction houses. Entire bedroom suites (dressing table, wardrobe, chest of drawers, chair and headboard) are still easy to find. Re-upholster them in glossy satin or velvet. Create a contemporary version of mirrored furniture by covering a simple shape with mirror mosaics or

'Where's the **man** who could **ease a heart** like **the satin** gown?'

Dorothy Parker

commission specially cut mirror pieces to cover a cut-out fibreboard shape (like the fan-shaped one on page 90).

soft furnishings

Sumptuous, sensual fabrics are key to this look. Revive all the most elaborate embellishments – buttoning, trimming, passementerie and elegant swagging. Round, rather than square, cushions were popular in the 1940s. Sheets should be silk satin and eiderdowns quilted. The softest Siberian goosedown pillows are covered in slippery silk pillowcases (less wrinkle-inducing than linen or cotton). Curtains are interlined to block out the light and muffle noise.

lights

Lighting the room presents another opportunity for decoration. Crystal-drop chandeliers and glass table lamps with beaded shades are the prettiest options. Wall sconces do not need to be wired for electric light; use candles instead – candlelight is so much more flattering to the skin.

storage

A decently proportioned, preferably 'walk-in', wardrobe is imperative for any glamourpuss. Divide and rule with endless compartments, tailor-made to house everything from lingerie to lipsticks. Storage experts can design a solution to streamline your hectic life. 'I've nothing to wear!' tantrums will become a thing of the past when all is perfectly hung in colour-coordinated rows.

how to live the high-maintenance life

- Frequent cocktail bars but never buy your own drinks
- Find a sugar daddy
- Wax everything
- Get Hollywood teeth
- Detox and Botox regularly
- Never leave the house without shades
- Always insist on an upgrade
- Take a taxi
- Be flighty
- Order off-menu
- Order in from your favourite restaurant
- Only diamonds will do

Baby doll

The baby doll never outgrew the 'Lolita' stage and her tastes haven't really evolved since puberty. She knows what she wants and pouts whenever she doesn't get it. For her, nothing beats good old-fashioned sulking. See her stamp her pedicured feet when it's not going her way; but like a spring shower, it's all over in an instant and she's soon purring appreciatively once again.

Graduating with honours from the Jayne Mansfield school of decorating, the baby doll is obsessed with pink, that most feminine of colours. Not just any old pink, mind you, she is hooked on the sugary sweet, candyfloss shade beloved of little girls. Shell pink, powder puff pink, rambling rose – the names alone send her into raptures. It certainly makes retail decisions easier; anything, as long as it's pink, will please her. Friends always know what to buy her for her birthday. 'I suppose that makes me a kind of minimalist,' she quips, fluttering an ostrich-feather fan. Thinking pink has given her whole life a direction. She is now branded; admirers see pink and immediately think of her. Thinkpink.com, now that's an idea ... Her car, mobile phone, Roberts Revival radio, fridge, toenails and lips are all in regulation pink. Even her pooch, Flossie, a tolerant West Highland terrier, has been known to make a rose-tinted exit from the poodle parlour.

The baby doll's sugar-coated boudoir is a monument to her girlhood (or, at least, the one she always dreamed about). Without a thought for practicality or comfort, she teeters about her home in feather-covered mules and a crepe de Chine slip while the heating is constantly set on 'high'.

style signature

Once upon a time the baby doll owned a Barbie doll's bedroom suite – a curvaceous white-and-gold plastic version of Louis Quinze. She lovingly decorated the bedroom in her favourite colour and accessorized it with romantic silk-taffeta drapes and satin bed linen, placed miniature scent bottles on the dressing table and filled tiny, doll-sized vases full of miniature roses. Born to modernist parents and brought up amid Scandinavian blond wood, she vowed to herself that one day she would re-create her own Barbie bedroom. To her, it represented just the sort of tasteless frivolity that was missing from the subtle, pared-down surroundings of her childhood.

Now the baby doll has her own faux Louis suite, which was made of painted wood in the 1950s, rather than white plastic. A soft shade of grey, it goes well with pink and has gold-leaf details, including her initials, imprinted on the crest of the carved headboard. She discovered someone who makes the most luxurious old-fashioned padded satin counterpanes, and going against the grain, opted for impractical, dazzling white. The baby doll sleeps between custom-made oyster-white Chinese silk sheets.

As for floors, at heart she's a wall-to-wall carpet kind of a girl, but somehow she couldn't resist placing a pink sheepskin rug on either side of the bed. Fitted cupboards line the wall opposite her bed and these are filled to bursting with frothy marabou-trimmed negligées and sweet little dresses. The doors, designed to pastiche Louis-style, are panelled and fitted with curly gilt handles.

Secret admirers ensure a constant supply of delicate posies. Sweet peas, her absolute favourite, elicit sighs of contentment, while bouquets of roses are marked down for lack of originality.

'Think pink!' is her mantra for living

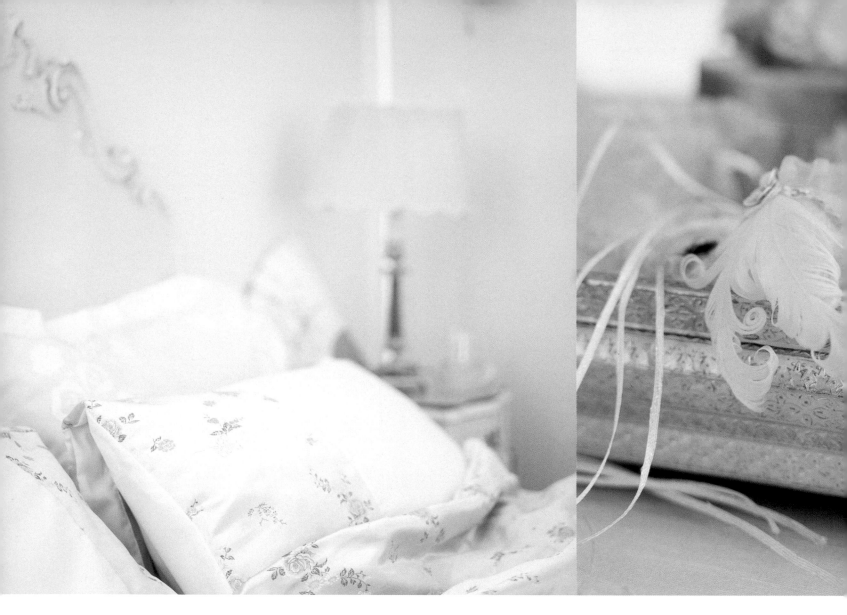

get the look

walls

The colour pink has long been associated with femininity. It was the favourite colour of Madame de Pompadour, Louis Quinze's long-term mistress, who introduced it into aristocratic Second Empire decorating. Jayne Mansfield's seminal baby doll home was a symphony in pink. There are endless variations on baby-pink paint; try a fresh shade that is neither too blue, nor too salmon. Stronger pinks can be much harder to live with. Wallpaper with a retro motif might also be appropriate – perhaps a small floral print with candy-coloured stripes.

furniture and accessories

Complete bedroom suites are easily found at auctions and in junk shops. The baby doll's headboard (see above left) has a bedside cabinet attached to it on each side, and the dressing table (see previous page) comes with a matching stool. Kitsch styling is intrinsic to the look – go as far over the top as you dare, with a curvaceous padded and buttoned headboard upholstered in something tactile like crushed velvet. Breakfast should be eaten in bed Barbara-Cartland style, off an original 1950s 'bed-tray' (on folding legs) set with rosebud china, delicate lace napkins and a silver teapot. The dressing table should

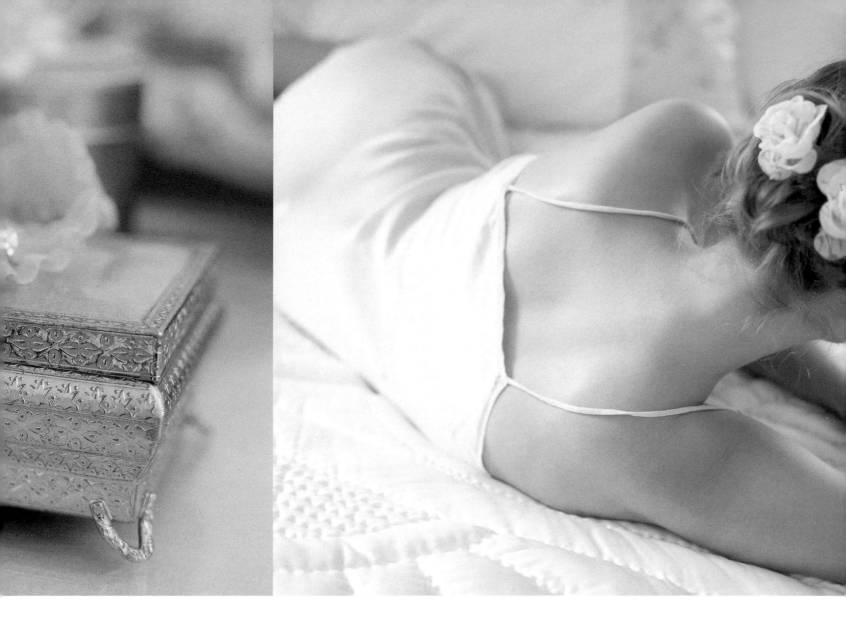

be smothered in all sorts of girlish trifles, and the triptych mirror decked in necklaces, ribbons, purses and scarves. Find a retro enamelled dressing-table set with matching hand-mirror, hair brushes, combs and ring box. As a finishing touch, arrange posies of pretty pink blooms in vintage Lalique glass vases.

A baby doll's boudoir needs a decorative screen for her to coyly undress behind, and plenty of pretty caskets to hold her jewels. Lampshades should be ruched and 'waisted' (charity shops are a great source for retro-shaped shades), and sometimes it's worth buying them just for their shape, as you can easily re-cover them.

soft furnishings

Camp it up a bit in true baby-doll style with short and full windowsill-length curtains and fabric-covered pelmets on everything from the bed to the dressing table and stool, all decorated with old-fashioned bobbled trimmings. All the fabrics you use should be slightly 'tacky' – choose shiny satins, damasks, velvets and silks. Add trimmings to round cushions and experiment with pleating, ruching and quilting.

accessories

Think kitsch and reinstate retro styles for accessories. Anything with fluffy feathers and delicate flowers will fit the bill.

'Banish the black, burn the blue, and bury the beige, from now on girls, think pink.'

Funny Face

exotic

Hippie chick

What could be more natural than a free-thinking Indian camping out in the fresh air? A rolling stone who is more than happy to gather moss, the hippie chick is sticking as close to nature as she can. Her nirvana is a secret wood, lush with ferns and plenty of tall, silver birches, where she can pitch a tent, erect an awning or build her own treehouse. Literally 'grounded' by proximity to the earth, she relishes in the chance to stargaze at night. The wind in the trees, the birdsong and the scent of freshly-cut logs are all the sensual aphrodisiacs she needs.

Hers is a completely spontaneous approach to making a 'home' that has more to do with how she feels than with putting down roots in a particular country or place. The hippie chick's woodland idyll could be constructed anywhere, even inside a building. The main ingredients are pieces picked up on her pilgrimages to India and other parts of Asia. Hers is a totally transportable lifestyle. In her quest to be less attached to material possessions, she is more than likely to trade precious treasures with other travellers, or simply to give them away to new friends.

Resourceful and practical, the hippie chick would be the ideal person to be marooned with on a desert island. Not only would her shelter withstand tropical rains, it would also be beautiful – embellished with little pagan altars and still lifes of stones and driftwood – and the days would pass by rapidly. The hippie chick would acquaint herself with how to make the most of the local vegetation and the cleverest ways of catching fish. Nights would be spent weaving baskets out of palm leaves or working out astrological charts.

style signature

The hippie chick is not your average walking ethnic cliché, reeking of patchouli and clad in limp, tie-dye rags. She has a fresh take on Indian merchandise and avoids the rich colour palette of reds, oranges and ochres long-associated with ethnic decoration. This is an edited, restrained version of the look, using dusty pinks, duck-egg blues and silver.

> 'To **travel** hopefully is a **better** thing than to **arrive**.'
>
> **Robert Louis Stevenson**

Her most luxurious saris have been turned into pillowcases and cushion covers; some beaded with silver, others a patch-work of vintage pieces stitched together. Impromptu though it may be, the hippie chick's al fresco pad is as well-equipped and considered as any indoor scheme. She chooses a luxuriant spot, where tall trees provide anchoring points for structure. The floor is marked out with bamboo decking. Rattan screens define the head of the bed, but the rest of the outdoor 'room' remains open to the elements. From the trees, she suspends a frame made of bamboo poles. She slings a length of organza over it, more for effect than for protection from the elements, and hangs up lanterns.

Rough-hewn square wooden blocks, used as a table and incense-holder, add graphic modernity to the hippie chick's summer encampment. Naturally, everything is low-level and perfect for casual lounging.

get the look

flooring

Bamboo decking, inexpensive and durable, makes a sturdy base for the 'room' and can create different levels. Squares can usually be bought singly. Wooden decking, kilims, tatami mats and seagrass or coir rugs would also do the job.

furniture

The materials of the tropics – rattan, cane, bamboo, wicker, rush and palm leaves – are surprisingly strong and adaptable. Rattan screens, which can be left natural or painted, are perfect for making a temporary outdoor shelter and could also be used to line walls indoors.

   Little furniture is required. Roll-up rush mats can be layered to make a mattress and enormous palm-covered floor cushions provide seating. Folding wooden steamer chairs or loungers would fit into the scheme, as would a rope hammock slung between two trees. Among the lush greenery, a shocking-pink tasselled parasol provides a flash of glorious colour as well as shade.

soft furnishings

Bring opulence outdoors with layers of cosy silk quilts. Their lavish sheen contrasts with the rustic simplicity of natural materials. Long decorative saris are ripe for converting into covers for cushions, pillows and bolsters. If you are not a natural Robinson Crusoe, consider mosquito nets, wind-breaks and awnings, and other ready-made shelters available from camping stores.

lights

Hang storm lanterns made of tin and glass in groups from trees and plant wax flares in the earth to light a woodland idyll atmospherically. Keep mosquitoes and other bugs away with citronella-scented candles. At dusk, light a pathway to your encampment with a double row of brown paper bags filled with sand and illuminated with tea lights.

'Shocking pink
is the navy blue
of India.'

Diana Vreeland

how to

Bamboo is light, strong and inexpensive and makes the perfect frame for a tent.

1. Firmly embed four bamboo poles in the earth or sand to mark each corner of the tent.

2. Lay out six more poles in a grid formation on the ground to make the top frame. Bind them together at each join with twine or strong tape.

3. Attach the frame to the upright poles with more twine (you will need help to lift it into position).

4. Attach ready-made muslin or organza panels to the cross poles, or drape them with saris or exotic fabrics.

5. Suspend lanterns from the middle poles.

• Variation: On a smaller scale, a large garden parasol becomes a shady hideaway when you sew floor-length fabric to the ends of each spoke.

Oriental minimalist

The Oriental minimalist wants to retreat to an oasis of order and calm.
She is particularly drawn to symmetry, being so much more balanced and restful than its
antithesis. Her cool, calm and collected interior is decorated in a soothing palette of duck-
egg blue and cherry-blossom pink, inspired by watercolours. In Japan, cherry blossom is
admired with reverence and the Japanese even organize springtime blossom-viewing parties.
These short-lived but abundant flowers remind her of the frailty and transience of existence.
In her boudoir, she feels calm, unflustered, protected from the chaos of the outside world
and more able to live a quiet, reflective life.

She may seem serene, introverted and other-worldly, but the Oriental minimalist's approach
to life is both practical and spiritual. A deep respect for ritual attracted her to the sophistication
and refinement of the East. The tea ceremony, sado, which was developed by fifteenth-century
Buddhist priests, encapsulates her approach to life. About much more than just drinking tea,
the meditative gestures also demonstrate manners and etiquette, and she considers it exercise
for the soul. Methodical and measured, she absorbs all the finest Oriental traditions and is never
concerned that they really belong to a completely foreign culture.

style signature

Geometric harmony dominates the Oriental interior. Squares and rectangles appear everywhere – in windows, screens and other room divisions. Materials are simple and natural: wood, paper, bamboo and tatami matting. The Oriental minimalist's uncluttered rooms tend to have a few pieces of low-level furniture, creating a feeling of spaciousness. Cherry blossom, the symbol of spring, was the inspiration for her tranquil scheme. The most decorative element in her boudoir is a room divider: a hand-painted branch of blossom stretches across the panel behind a geometric grid, suggesting a window looking onto a Japanese garden. Her bed is an unadorned bamboo structure topped with a futon mattress. There are no undisciplined, undulating bed covers – all are pulled as tightly and precisely as a hospital bed. Light is diffused through discreetly embroidered grey organza lampshades on either side of her immaculate bed, on which rest piles of symmetrical, regimented pillows and cushions.

The Oriental minimalist harbours a weakness for some form of controlled ornamentation. She contrives still lifes of china cups, vases, rice bowls and branches laden with blossom. These simple, everyday items become sophisticated when organized into groups. Storage, key to the minimalist interior, is hidden by seamless wall panels fitted with push-release catches. The balanced symmetry of the room has a hypnotic effect on visitors. They cannot help but feel revived by the ordered atmosphere, and resolve to eliminate their clutter as soon as they return home.

A wise Oriental minimalist consults a feng shui master before planning her layout. This ancient Eastern wisdom has it that if you harmonize the relationship between people and their environment, then health, wealth and happiness will follow.

'restraint and economy'

the Oriental minimalist's mantra

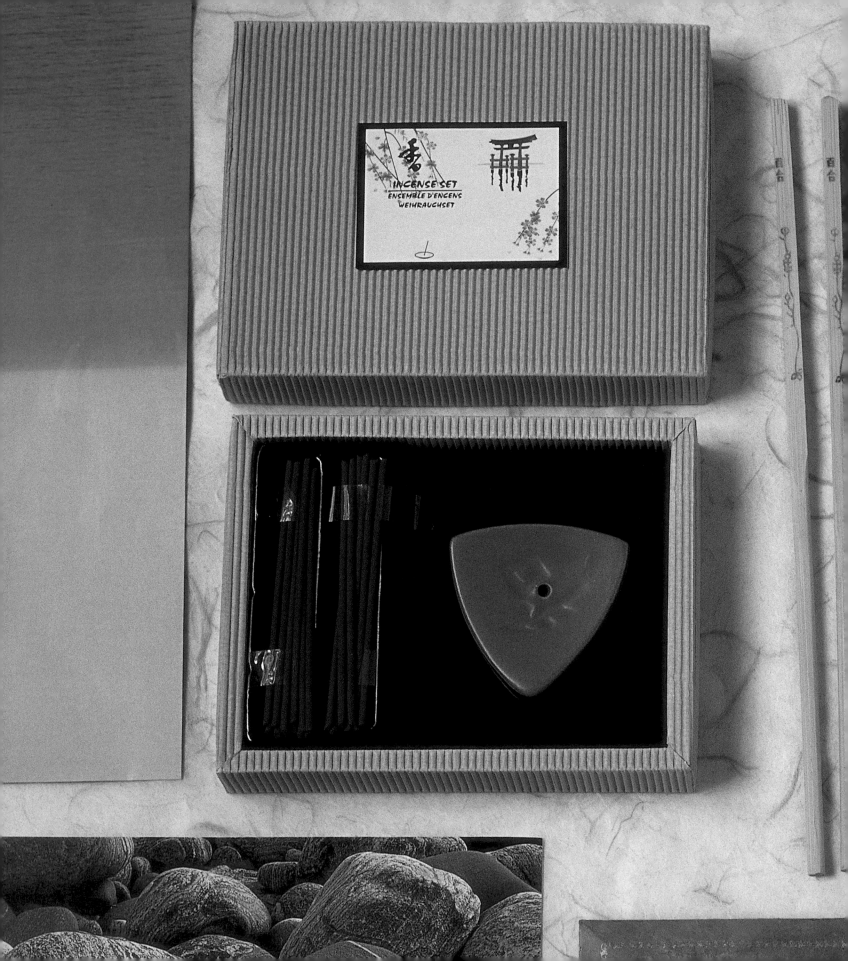

'The Japanese **mind** has always reminded me of the Japanese **garden**, which is a place that nature plainly **made** but which man has just as plainly **ordered**.'

Donald Richie, *The Inland Sea*

get the look

windows

In fastidiously minimal Japanese homes, the windows are
often sliding wooden screens 'glazed' with opaque paper.
Imitate the softly diffused light with tracing paper used either
as a roller blind or secured to glass panes with spray glue.
A permanent effect with etching paste can be achieved.

furniture

Very little furniture is needed to create this look – a futon,
with or without a base and perhaps raised on a platform
covered with tatami mats, along with a low table, stool
or console. Go for straight lines and pale colours. Almost
invisible, Perspex has the appropriate 'light' feel. Consider
pieces that can be dual purpose: the beech console here
works as a dressing table and as a display for ikebana skills.

soft furnishings

The windows in the boudoir of a pure devotee of Oriental minimalism need only be the plainest sheer organza panels or blinds, which allow the light to filter through and cast grid-patterned shadows of the windowpanes onto the walls and floors. Arranged in neat, ordered stacks, Oriental-style cushions are tighter and more disciplined than the Western variety. Hard and tightly-stuffed square or rectangular cushions, like miniature mattresses, are the perfect choice for kneeling on at a low table.

accessories

The low table is formally set with rice bowls, sake cups, chopsticks and votive candles. Single exotic stems suit austere vessels like slim, rectangular vases or tall crackle-glazed vases. Think symmetry and buy in pairs. The graphic, cylindrical storm lanterns, left, echo the grid of the screen.

China girl

The China girl is the mistress of controlled excess. She's a minimalist with maximalist tendencies; she loves order and restraint, but she's also mad about bold colour and exotic textures. Her two contradictory selves are at home in her splendid boudoir: a pared-down shell bursting with clashing shades and sumptuous fabrics. Happily, the tension works for her and not against her. She will search endlessly for exactly the right modern lacquer furniture, keeping polaroids of possible candidates and meticulous records of where she has been. Then she'll fall madly in love with a wildly expensive beaded shawl that she simply must have.

The flip side of the China girl's character would love to mooch around in bed all day with the blinds down, while her sensible self rises at 7 am, flings open the windows and takes a deep breath of air. It was impossible for her to decide which silk lantern to buy, so she took all of them home to consider suspending them in a line from the ceiling. She kept every one (her flip side was too lazy to return them).

The China girl suffers from irrational and terrible crushes: on men, a certain shade of shocking pink, and also the fat, ruby-red peonies that you can only buy once a year. The solution to her obsessive, compulsive crushes is to wait as long as is humanly possible before making a purchase. If the must-have item haunts her dreams continually for a specific period and is not superseded in the retail hierarchy by something more compelling, then, much to everyone's relief, she buys it. She knows all the assistants at her favourite boutiques by their first names and some unlucky ones tremble when she breezes in. They are already anticipating a long session of passion alternating with indecision, which will test their selling skills to the max.

style signature

The dramatic combination of black and red could so easily become an Oriental design cliché, but in the China girl's hands, and with the addition of clashing fuchsia pink, it seems original and contemporary. Instead of bordello chic, the China girl manages to contrive a sense of rich minimalism, a strange contradictory tension. She selects masculine, graphic shapes, which could otherwise look rather stern, but piles on plenty of exciting hot colours and diverse textures. A bold abstract painting, composed of intense blocks of red and pink with flashes of gold leaf, suggested the scheme. In China, where it is considered to be the colour of contentment, red has good overall connotations. Western experts argue that crimson is the worst shade to use in a bedroom, believing that it encourages sleeplessness, bad dreams and anger. The China girl compromises by keeping the walls white and accessorizing the space in the brightness of crimson.

'More is less, less is more' is the essence of the China girl

Instead of dowry chests and opium beds, the China girl breaks with tradition by choosing chunky cubes and rectangles in updated glossy lacquer as furniture, and a bed made of cardboard. An ingenious concertina construction, framed by glossy black lacquer cubes and rectangles, it is nattily dressed in crisp bands of silk and formal piles of pillows.

get the look

walls

If you are feeling very daring (more like China girl's alter ego, in fact), go dark and sultry and opt for a shade of nearly black, jet or slate grey; or go all the way and slap on a coat of liquorice gloss paint. The room in which you sleep can afford a gloomy, yet sensual vibe. Otherwise, for a less bold statement, stick to a clean, crisp, stark white, which always teams up smartly with reds, pinks and blacks. For a decadent touch, cover an entire wall in gold leaf, which will warm up the whole room beautifully.

floors

Hard, plain, industrial-style surfaces are in keeping with the pared-down, minimal aesthetic. The best options are ultra-groovy polished concrete, utilitarian rubber or hard-wearing floor paint. This is a good option if you already have wooden floorboards – simply give them an Eastern treatment with coats of shiny black floor paint sealed with several layers of varnish.

Alternatively, for those who prefer to have warmer, softer surfaces beneath their feet, the plainest, sleekest, short-pile carpet you can find in crimson or black will fit the bill perfectly.

furniture

Track down a contemporary bed with an Eastern twist. It should be low and unadorned, and topped with a futon mattress. If the traditionalist in you is screaming to be heard, there is a lot of imported Chinese lacquer furniture around, some of which is inexpensive. Achieve a minimal, Eastern look with sleek lacquer cubes that form part of a modular range, which can be stacked and reconfigured as storage. Take tea at a low ebony table, or loll around in a folding black bamboo chair. A screen is always a useful prop in any boudoir; you can undress artfully behind it or use it to conceal unsightly heaps of clothes.

accessories

Assemble sculptural still lifes composed of traditional Chinese objects such as gold-leaf lacquer vases and ebony tea caddies, and add vibrancy with a single ravishing bloom placed in a ceramic cup. String up a mass of gorgeous silk or paper lanterns, which can be wired up with strands of electric fairy lights. Drape the bed with exotic silks and add neat piles of pillows. Keep the palette bold but restrained, sticking mainly to shades of red, pink and black for coherency. A beautiful teapot, a set of shiny lacquer trays, a caddy of green tea leaves, a pink suede neck pillow, a scarlet satin dressing gown and sequinned black velvet flip-flops all belong on the China girl's must-have list.

basic feng shui

Consider this traditional Eastern practice when you are designing the layout of your bedroom. Here are a few basic pointers to keep in mind.

• **Don't** sleep on a second-hand mattress. All soft furnishings absorb 'chi' (energy) and you don't want to deal with a predecessor's residual 'energy', do you?

• **Don't** hoard clutter underneath your bed. It prevents the flow of chi.

• **Do** encourage loving, harmonious partnerships by displaying objects and ornaments in pairs.

• **Don't** keep a mirror in your boudoir. If you do, cover it while you sleep.

• **Don't** paint your bedroom red. It will disturb your sleep.

• **Do** encourage chi to flow during the day by opening a window.

• **Don't** watch television in bed. The electro-magnetic field affects the quality of your sleep.

Spice girl

Some like it hot – the spice girl does – hot colours, hot climates, hot food. She longs to lounge in far-flung places that are heady with incense, listening to rai music and sipping mint tea. And she does, in her make-believe souk and tented bower. She brings the exotic home with her, dragging carpets, ceramics, glass, textiles and even native drums through customs. The spice girl never shops in department stores; her kind of retail therapy takes place in markets and kasbahs. It is the whole experience that counts, not simply buying a suitable rug. She is very fond of commissioning craftsmen to make things to her particular requirements. It gives her something to do on holiday (but she never holidays, she travels), and she always needs to have a project.

The spice girl's den is an inspired fusion of Asian, North African and Mediterranean characteristics. Instead of being a mere copyist, she absorbs a style and makes it her own. The spice girl is happiest lolling around on the floor or on low-level outsized cushions; structure just isn't for her. She is the sort of girl who never wears shoes and always makes a point of sitting on the floor, even at great- aunt Maud's. She harbours drawers full of beads and tea chests crammed with saris, kilims and pashminas. Whenever wanderlust overwhelms her, she examines her booty from past journeys and re-reads travel diaries that are plastered with ethnic confectionery wrappers, sketches, local aphorisms and bus tickets. She is expert at re-creating exotic fantasies catering for all the senses: a spice girl will scent her home with incense and essential oils, and serve you *chai* or mint tea that you drink from a special glass or weirdly shaped pot. She will insist on pronouncing foreign words correctly with an impeccable accent.

style signature

The spice girl is fearless about colour and mixes her own paints from pigments bought abroad. Bold, brash shades are the best antidote to grey skies that she knows. She has a can-do attitude to decoration and eagerly takes on projects to mosaic a floor, dip-dye her curtains or create imitation stained-glass on her windows.

The spice girl's scheme begins with a sumptuous silk cushion – embroidered, beaded and be-ribboned. It is a combination of several precious pieces of fabric expertly stitched together, and she builds up the colour story around this improbable mixture of raspberry pink, scarlet, turquoise and orange. Her bed is just a mattress or futon, nothing too formal or permanent (she likes to think of herself as itinerant and her nomadic furniture must be easy to move). The room rustles with lush layers of silk and organza over the bed as a canopy made from a semi-sheer sari pinned to the ceiling at exactly the right length to skim the floor. There is something about her boudoir that is reminiscent of an Eastern harem. As a small girl, she dreamt of living in the equivalent of an Alma-Tadema painting; all languorous Pre-Raphaelite maidens swathed in Fortuny pleated robes, reclining on silken benches and telling Scheherezade-style tales of love and adventure.

The floor is a patchwork of rugs, thick-pile woollen *gabbehs* and rougher kilims. If she could afford it, she might splash out on leather floor tiles which would improve with age. Seasonal changes inspire her to alter the mood of the room, using, for example, darker, richer colours in winter with heavier fabrics and headier scents.

'God is in the details' is her mantra for living

get the look

walls

Remember, the look is more Luis Barragan than themed restaurant walls. Try pigment rubbed into raw plaster walls in shades reminiscent of Mexican pueblos – turquoise, pink and ochre. A bright colour used on just one wall is less overwhelming in a small space. Textiles can be hung on walls and floors and across spaces to create a private enclosure within a room.

True nomads get out their staple guns and attempt a fabric-lined boudoir. Simply frame the four walls by fitting wooden battens to the edges and then cover the walls with lengths of fabric, stretching it tight and stapling it in place. Canvas, dyed muslin or saris are ideal fabrics to use. An entire wall covered in gold, copper or bronze leaf would add a touch of luxury and contrast to the simpler, rougher textures and raw, earthy colours.

floors

Low-level lounging requires warm and comfortable flooring. Traditional kilims are flat-woven and usually geometrically patterned, and the colours are muted (make sure not to mix too many carpets together or your boudoir will look like a souk). Plain rugs with pile are definitely a much more comfortable option. The fuchsia-pink and white striped rug (see pages 132–3) adds a contemporary edge to an ethnic look. Printed fake cowhide (a zebra or pony print) gives the spice girl's den a wild safari style and animalistic feel that is both modern and ethnic.

how to

• Earth pigments can be
rubbed directly into still-
wet freshly plastered
walls or mixed into wet
plaster before application.

• Dilute the pigment with
water and add it to water-
based paint, drop by
drop, until you achieve
the desired colour.

• For a sheeny finish,
sprinkle powder into
beeswax and polish
it into the raw plaster.

furniture

All that is required is a mattress and some floor cushions or beanbags – the more relaxed and less structured the style, the better. Ottomans, tea chests and trunks provide excellent storage. Alternatively, build a long, low bench like a blanket box in a corner or along a wall and top it with upholstered cushions. North African buildings include many built-in features, such as benches and pillars, arched alcoves and storage cubbyholes, which are painted the same colour as the walls to create an impression of seamlessness. All the furniture in the room should be low – all the better for lounging.

soft furnishings

A spice den relies on the clever use of fabric to conjure up an exotic atmosphere. Extravagant fabrics can be found as close to home as a local market (try Asian establishments for saris). The choice is endless – plains in shocking colours, diaphanous glittery sheers or embroidered crewelwork.

Some kind of tent effect, either over the entire room or just a simple canopy over the bed, immediately softens the space, and a fabric tent or screen defines a sleeping area. Ready-made muslin or organza panels with ties can be hung on a bamboo frame suspended from the ceiling around the bed, or just use drawing pins (thumbtacks) to hold up a sari. Mounds of cushions in every conceivable shape and size add to the comfort factor.

windows

Instead of curtains, consider shutters or pierced and lacy metal grills. The Moors integrated precise interlaced designs into their architecture, and delicately worked screens allow privacy yet allow light to filter through and cast intricate shadows.

lights

Light your den with a collection of lanterns, such as glass-jewelled brass globes with star-shaped cut-outs, organza concertina lanterns, tin storm lanterns or lustrous silk balloon shapes. For pools of candlelight, place rose-scented candles in Moroccan tea glasses.

ddress book

Alma Home
12–14 Greatorex Street
London E1 5NF
Tel: (020) 7377 0762
www.almahome.co.uk
(A company who design and produce
leather and suede furniture and products
for the home)

Babylon Design
301 Fulham Road
London SW10 9QH
Tel: (020) 7376 7255
info@babylondesign.demon.co.uk
(Interior design, furniture and
home products)

The Blue Door
74 Church Road
London SW13 0DQ
Tel: (020) 8748 9785
(Interior design company specializing in
the Gustavian period; supplier of Swedish
furniture and textiles; furniture made and
handpainted to order)

BowWow
70 Princedale Road
London W11 4NL
Tel: (020) 7792 8532
(Contemporary furniture, paintings, ceramics,
soft furnishings and turned objects)

Carden Cunietti
83 Westbourne Park Road
London W2 5QH
Tel: (020) 7229 8630
www.carden-cunietti.com
(Home interiors and women's accessories)

The Cross
141 Portland Road
London W11 4LR
Tel: (020) 7727 6760
www.thecrosscatalogue.com
(Houseware, clothing and accessories)

J & M Davidson
47 Ledbury Road
London W11 2AB
Tel: (020) 7313 9532
(Home section, bags, leather goods,
knitwear and outerwear)

Dulux Advice Centre
Tel: (01753) 550 555
(General enquiries on paint and products)

Ella Doran
Unit H
Ground Floor South
95–7 Redchurch Street
London E2 7DJ
Tel: (020) 7613 0782
www.elladoran.co.uk
(Interior accessories)

Ena Green Antiques
566 King's Road
London SW6 2DY
Tel: (020) 77362485
(Nineteenth- and twentieth-century English
and Continental painted furniture)

The General Trading Company
144 Sloane Street
London SW1X 9BL
Tel: (020) 7730 0411
www.gen-trading.co.uk
(Furniture and accessories)

Graham & Green
4, 7 & 10 Elgin Crescent
London W11 2JA
Tel: (020) 7727 4594
www.graham&green.co.uk
(Home furnishings, ceramics, clothing
and kitchenware)

IKEA
Tel: (020) 8208 5607
(Houseware and accessories. Phone for
general enquiries and store locations)

Immaculate House
4–5 Burlington Arcade
London W1V 9AB
Tel: (020) 7499 5758
(Handmade natural soaps, gifts and
products for interiors)

Jacqueline Edge
1 Court Nell Street
London W2 5BU
Tel: (020) 7229 1172
Also at:
The Old Barns
Manor Farm
Chilmark
Wiltshire SP3 5AS
Tel: (01722) 717 800
www.i.-i.net/jacquelineedge.com
(Imported goods for house and garden
from Burma and Vietnam)

Josephine Ryan Antiques
63 Abbeville Road
London SW4 9JW
Tel: 020 8675 3900
(French distressed and painted furniture
and accessories, including mercury
silver and chandeliers)

Judy Greenwood Antiques
657 Fulham Road
London SW6 5PY
Tel: (020) 7736 6037
(Decorative French furniture and accessories
from the nineteenth and twentieth centuries)

Kara Kara
2a Pond Place
London SW3 6QJ
Tel: (020) 7591 0891
(Range of handcrafted Japanese artefacts)

Lakeland Limited
Alexander Buildings
Windermere
Cumbria LA23 1BQ
Tel: (01539) 488 100
www.lakelandlimited.com
(Storage items)

Minh Mang
182 Battersea Park Road
London SW11 4ND
Tel: (020) 7498 3233
Minhmang@lineone.net
(Vietnamese and Cambodian silks
for interiors and fashion)

Mint
70 Wigmore Street
London W1H 9DL
Tel: (020) 7224 4406
(Interiors and lifestyle accessories)

Ogier
177 Westbourne Grove
London W11 2SB
Tel: (020) 7229 0783
Ogier@dircon.co.uk
(French and English complementary
living designs, including artefacts,
furniture, accessories, sculptures,
screens, tables and lighting)

Paint Library
5 Ellystan Street
London SW3 3NT
(020) 7823 7755
www.paintlibrary.co.uk
(Paints including David Oliver, David Oliver
architectural colours and Nina Campbell)

Paperchase Products Limited
12 Alfred Place
London WC1E 7EB
Tel: 020 7467 6200
rite@paperchase.co.uk
(Range of paper products
including handmade)

Pimpernel & Partners
596 King's Road
London SW6 2DX
Tel: (020) 7731 2448
(French country antiques)

Purves & Purves
80–81 & 83 Tottenham Court Road
London W1P 9DH
Tel: (020) 7580 8223
www.purves.co.uk
(Contemporary furniture, rugs, lighting
and household accessories)

Retro Home
20 Pembridge Road
London W11 3HO
Tel: (020) 7221 2055
www.buy/sell/trade.co.uk
(Retro furniture and accessories)

Sanderson
100 Acres
Sanderson Road
Uxbridge
Middlesex UB8 1DH
Tel: (01895) 251 288
www.sanderson-uk.com
(Paints, wallpapers, soft furnishings
and furniture)

Skandium
72 Wigmore Street
London W1H 9DL
(020) 7935 2077
www.skandium.com
(Scandinavian furniture and glassware)

Space
214 Westbourne Grove
London W11 2RH
Tel: (020) 7229 6533
(Lifestyle store)

Stepan Tertsakian Limited
64 Queen Street
London EC4R 1AD
Tel: (020) 7236 8788
(Animal hides and rugs)

Twelve
31 Hornsey Road
London N7 7DD
Tel: (020) 7686 0773
www.twelvelimited.com
(Mail-order company that specializes in
reclaimed and recycled pieces; also furniture
designed and made to commission)

Twentytwentyone
274 Upper Street
London N1 2UA
Tel: 020 7288 1996
(Range of classic twentieth-century furniture,
including designs by Charles Eames and
Verner Panton)

Urban Outfitters
36–8 Kensington High Street
London W8 4PH
Tel: (020) 7761 1001
(Kitschy home accessories and clothing)

Vessel
114 Kensington Park Road
London W11 2PW
Tel: 020 7727 8001
(Ceramics, glass and stainless steel vessels
from individual designers and large
companies; five annual exhibitions)

V V Rouleaux Limited
6 Marylebone High Street
London W1M 3PB
Tel: (020) 7224 5179
www.vvrouleaux.com
(Ribbons, braids, cords and tie-backs)

X-Film UK Limited
Freephone: 0800 731 6134
(Self-adhesive vinyl)

$\mathcal{B}$ibliography

Quotation Sources

p. 16 Mitford, Nancy, *Love in a Cold Climate*, London, Penguin Classics, 1990

p. 31 Mansfield, Katherine, *Prelude* in *Bliss and Other Stories* (Wordsworth Collection, Modern Classics), London, Penguin, 1999

p. 43 Smith, Dodie, *I Capture the Castle*, London, Virago Press, 1998

p. 46 Honoré de Balzac, as quoted in Ypma, Herbert, *Paris: Objet Trouvé*, London, Thames & Hudson, 1996

p. 48 Ypma, Herbert, *Paris: Objet Trouvé*, London, Thames & Hudson, 1996

p. 65 Friedrich Nietzsche, as quoted in Crawford, Ilse, *Sensual Home*, London, Quadrille, 1997

p. 73 Jessica Rabbit, *Who Framed Roger Rabbit*, directed by Robert Zemeckis, 1988

p. 75 Carter, Angela, *The Loves of Lady Purple* in *Bad Girls and Wicked Women*, London, Virago Press, 1986

p. 90 Dorothy Parker, *The Satin Dress*, 1937

p100 *Funny Face*, directed by Stanley Dohen, 1956

p107 Robert Louis Stevenson, Virginibus Puerisque, 1881

p110 Diana Vreeland

p. 119 Richie, Donald, *The Inland Sea*, London, Kodansha International, 1993

Further Reading

Calloway, Stephen, *Baroque Baroque: The Culture of Excess*, London, Phaidon Press, 1994

Crawford, Ilse, *Sensual Home*, London, Quadrille, 1997

Cumberbatch, Jane, *Pure Style*, London, Ryland, Peters and Small, 1996

Dilcock, Lesley, *Global Style*, London, Ryland, Peters and Small, 2000

Edwards, Jane, *Asian Elements: Natural Balance in Eastern Living*, London, Conran Octopus, 1999

Hall, Dinah, *Country and Modern*, London, Quadrille, 1998

Norden, Mary, *Modern Country*, London, Contran Octopus, 2000

Ympa, Herbert, *Mexican Contemporary*, London, Thames & Hudson, 1997

Picture Credits

The publishers would like to thank the following sources for their kind permission to reproduce the pictures in this book:

Tom Leighton 37, 38tl, 38bl, 39, 40l, 40r, 41, 42l, 42tr, 42br, 43, 44, 45, 46, 47, 48, 49, 50tl, 50bl, 50br, 51, 96, 97, 98l, 98r, 99, 100bl, 100br, 101, 122, 124, 126, 127, 128tl, 128bl, 128br, 129.

David Loftus 5, 6, 87, 88, 89, 90, 91, 92, 93tr, 93br.

Mel Yates 2, 3, 4, 8, 18, 19, 20, 21, 22tr, 22tl, 23, 24, 25, 26, 28, 29, 30, 31, 32, 33, 34tl, 34bl, 34br, 35t, 35b, 54, 56, 57l, 57r, 58tl, 58tr, 58br, 59, 60l, 60r, 61, 62, 64, 65, 66rl, 66bl, 67, 68, 69tl, 69tr, 69br, 70, 71, 72, 73, 74tr, 74bl, 75tl, 75br, 77, 78, 79bl, 79tr, 80/81, 82, 83, 84, 85bl, 85br, 85tr, 94, 100tl, 105, 106, 107, 108tr, 108tl, 109, 110tl, 110tr, 110bl, 111tr, 111br, 111bl, 112, 114, 115, 116, 118, 119tr, 119br, 120tl, 120bl, 120r, 121bl, 121tr, 121br, 130, 132, 134, 135, 136l, 136r, 137tr, 137br, 138tl, 138cl, 138bl, 138tr, 138br, 139t, 139b.

Elizabeth Zeschin 1, 11, 12, 13tr, 13br, 14, 15, 16tl, 16bl, 17.

Every effort has been made to acknowledge correctly and contact the source and/or copyright holder of each picture, and Carlton Books Limited apologises for any unintentional errors or omissions which will be corrected in future editions of this book.

$\mathscr{A}$cknowledgements

Many thanks to Venetia Penfold and the 'Pink Team'
at Carlton Books for their encouragement, amusing
gossip and support. Also to Mel Yates, photographer,
and assistant Jake, for their unfailing patience, good
humour and quite nice pictures.

I am eternally grateful to all the suppliers in my address
book, especially to Sue Mackworth-Praed at Graham &
Green and Pauline at L'Accademia Antiques.

Thanks to Souki Hildreth for turning out to be the
perfect person to assist me and to my trusty van
drivers for their efficiency.

Finally, I must thank my mother, Pamela Robertson,
for passing on her shopping genes and giving me
such a thorough retail training.

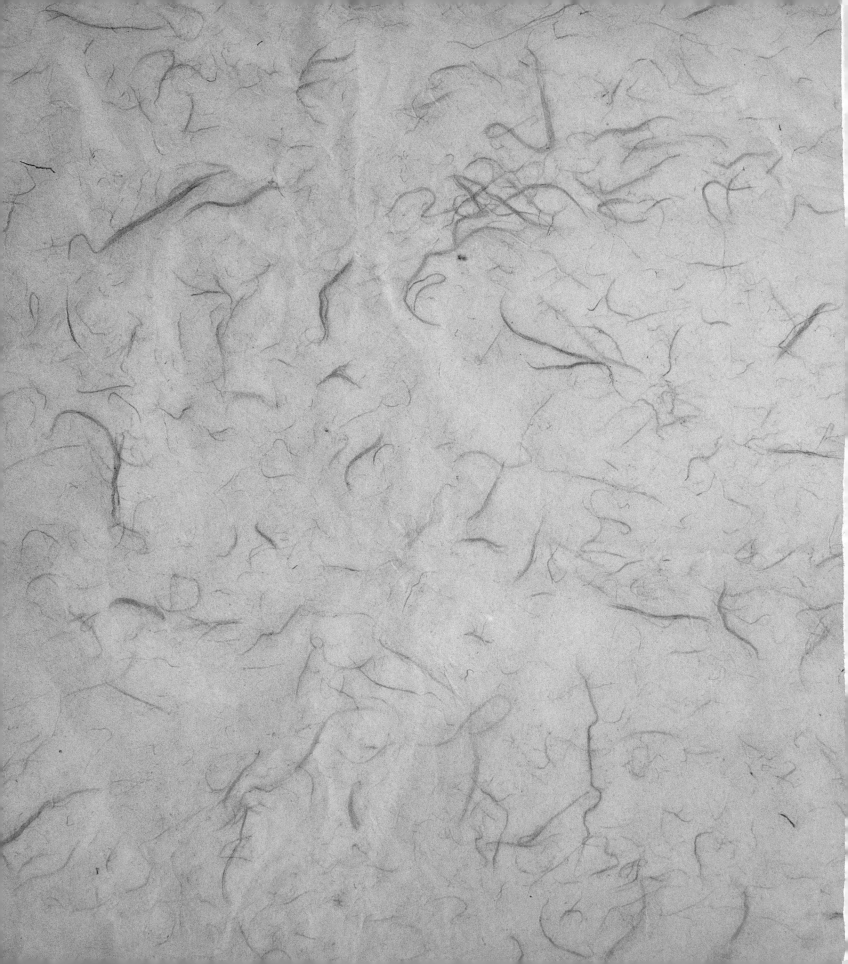